Making Friends in Business

Big Dreams

•

Big Risks

•

Big Faith

•

Big Success

by:
Helen Overly

Making Friends in Business

Library of Congress Control Number:	2016954357
ISBN-13: Paperback:	978-1-63524-432-8
PDF:	978-1-63524-433-5
ePub:	978-1-63524-434-2
Kindle:	978-1-63524-435-9
Hardcover:	978-1-63524-436-6

Printed in the United States of America

LitFire
PUBLISHING

LitFire LLC
1-800-511-9787
www.litfirepublishing.com
order@litfirepublishing.com

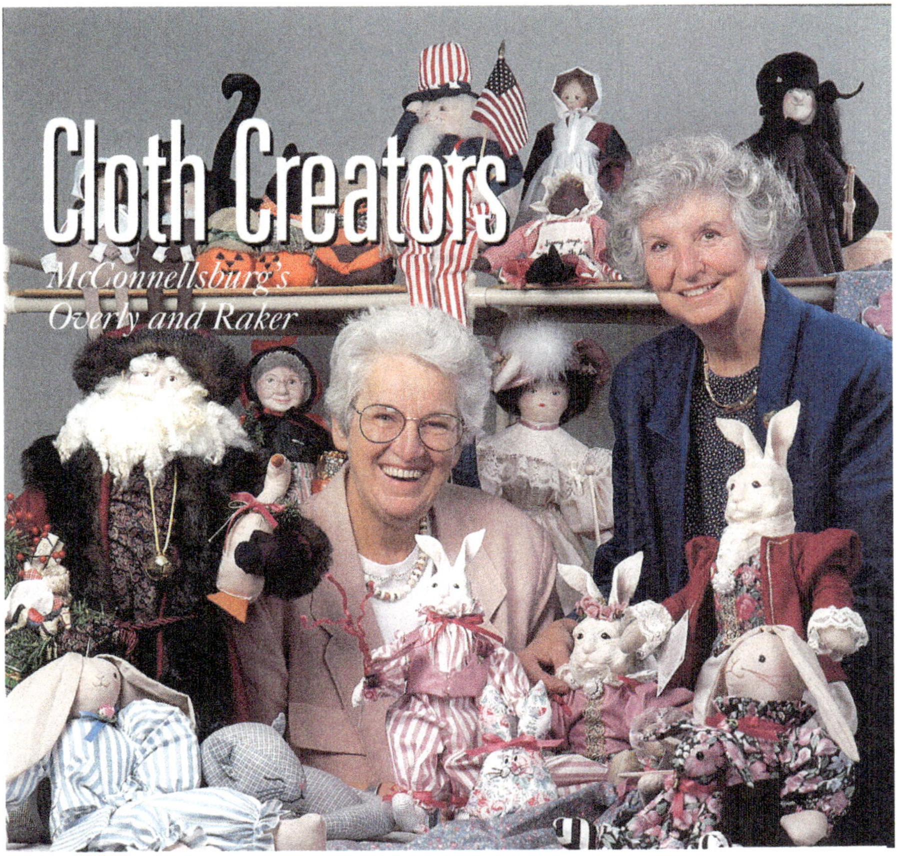

Two Brave Hearts on the Road to Success...

CONTENTS

This book is dedicated to

Freda Mae Raker,

without whose creative genius and faithful, loving friendship this book could not exist.

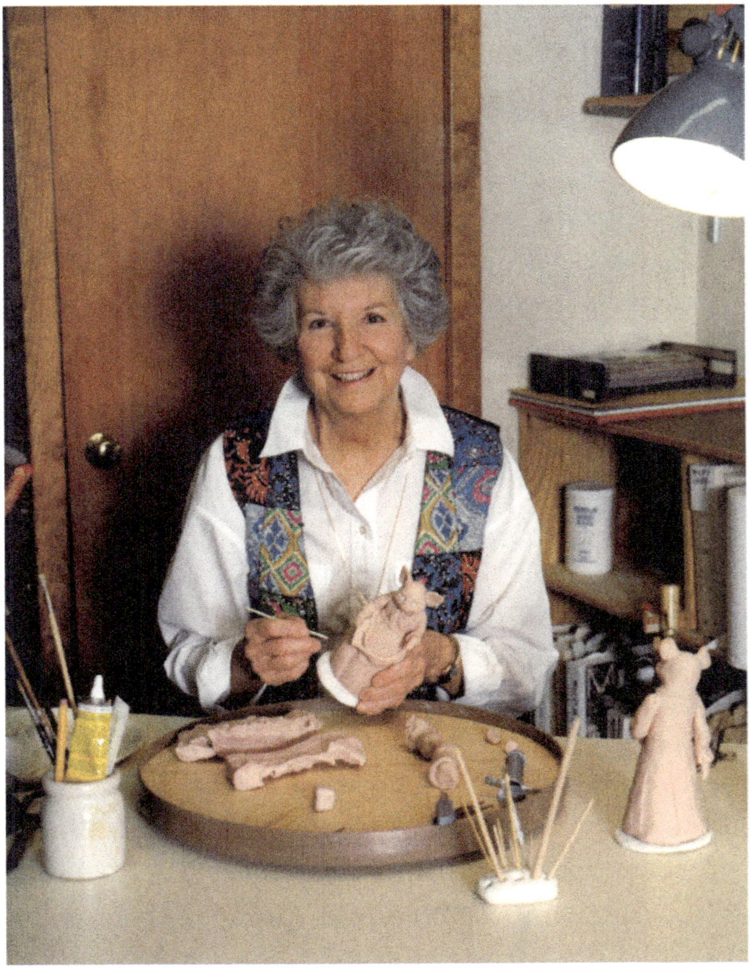

ACKNOWLEDGMENTS

For many years, after talking about our business, its growth, and the funny things that happened along the way, I have heard hundreds of times, "You ought to write a book."

After thinking about it, probably for years, I finally decided I just might do it. Well, here it is!

Two people, Angie Zinobile and Linda Barling, have been relentless in urging me into action.

Another big nudge came when I met Susanne Reed, who herself had written two books. I felt a little better about taking the plunge since I now knew someone with some book-writing experience. Her firsthand knowledge has been invaluable. She has guided me through difficult spots when I came to some stalemates. It was not the writing that was difficult, but how to put it altogether in some semblance of order.

I tried to keep this writing project a secret just in case I never finished it. However, I did share this quiet idea with two other special friends, Marcella Wachtel and Mary Rizzo-Bonney, both who encouraged me and helped me with editing, a laborious job. Mary spent many days with me helping put the book in final order, tweaking the manuscript here and there and finally assisting me with deciding on photos, their placements, and overall signing off on the final document. Not sure this would have been done without Mary.

The cover! The last thing to be done. Who would have ideas and creative ability to do the cover? A relative of Freda's! Of course, Julie Chamberlain Norris, a graphic artist who once worked for us. What a blessing to have Julie design and expedite this cover.

I must admit all these folks pushed (maybe even shoved) me along the way. Finally, when I was struggling with writing the very the end of the book, another close friend, Dinah Chamberlain, said, "Why don't you end with Habakkuk, your story of faith that you talk about?" I did it!

A very special thanks to these folks, along with the many others who have put up with me telling the stories that are now down in black and white.

We are blessed with a large, loving extended family. Too many to name, and some are missing from this photo.

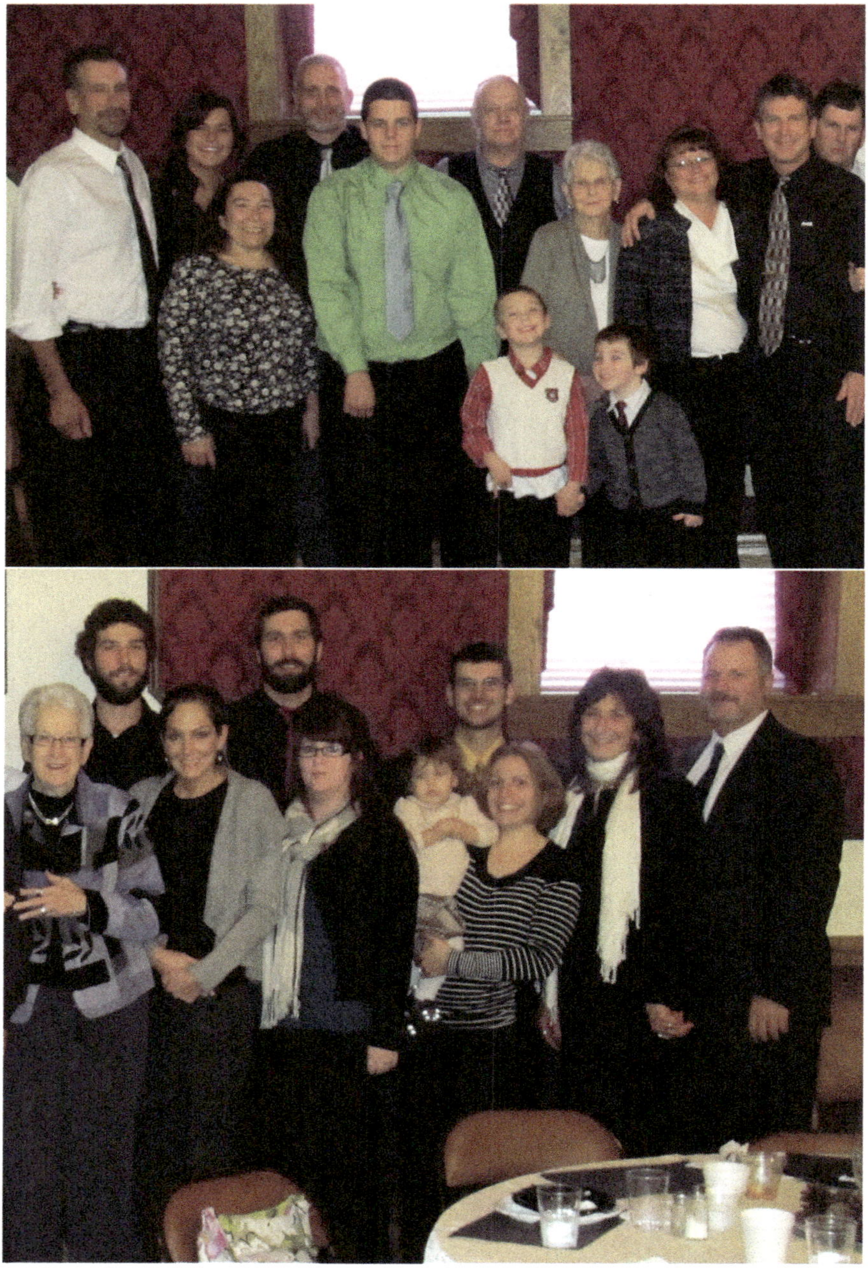

INTRODUCTION

My wish for the reader is simple.

I want to entertain you, inspire you, give you hope, and build your faith.

What is your passion?

What is keeping you from your dream?

What would you like to accomplish but fear holds you captive?

What kinds of fear? What are the issues?

If there were no financial risk, no threat of failure, but being absolutely assured you will succeed, what will you do? Again the question, what is your passion? What would you really like to do?

This can be you!

"In order to grow, you have to let go."

Be inspired by the business achievement recorded in this book.

If you have a desire or a dream to do something, do it! Don't just talk about it; make it happen. Don't worry about all the things you don't know. Not knowing can be a blessing. When problems arise, don't give up. Work until a solution is found. Hard work? Yes, but exciting to see your dream coming true every day.

Two rather unlikely candidates for the business world put together a retail and wholesale manufacturing business. Before the journey concluded, they would generate millions of dollars in sales, battle an archaic state law, and traverse the globe.

An exciting story of two single women ages forty-two and forty-seven who quit successful jobs to travel out into the unknown, making friends.

Taking a risk? That too, but having faith. Seeing what God will do with lots of hope, fortitude, and never thinking of giving up. Bumps and challenges along the way? Oh yes, but that is even more faith building. Keep a positive attitude, and never give up!

CHAPTER 1

Faith, Prayer, and Blastoff

> The success of Overly-Raker is a story that goes beyond creativity and clever marketing. It's about fearlessness, drive, and diversity.
>
> —Franca Lewis, *Herald-Mail*

Would you be brave enough to start a business on a dried mushroom? Sounds crazy, but that is exactly what started the success story of two single women whose creativity and hard work led to products marketed throughout the United States and Europe.

Who were these wild (friends thought irresponsible) ladies who would give up the perks of good jobs and benefits to launch out into the unknown? Who were these brave women who took the giant risk of quitting their jobs and moving to the country (McConnellsburg, Pennsylvania) with only the dream of producing a gift catalog with handmade items and opening a tiny retail store in the basement of the new home just built and moved into?

Well, I will tell you.

Freda Raker was an executive secretary working for the plant manager of DuPont's largest chemical plant, located in Deep Water, New Jersey. She had worked at DuPont for twenty-two years. Freda was a very creative and multitalented lady. While she had a prestigious job, her artistic talent was just waiting to explode. While living and working in New Jersey, she used her spare time to design social notes and to paint the local historical scenes, in beautiful watercolor renditions. Most of those early paintings were given as gifts, but here and there, she sold a few.

I, Helen Overly, was a teacher in a school at Penns Grove, New Jersey. I taught science and math in the seventh and eighth grades. My talent was not so much in the artistic venue but in working in the community and always looking for ways to showcase Freda's work. Sales would be my forte.

Looking back, I think that we really were a bit crazy. Freda was forty-seven years old, and I had just turned forty-two. As I signed my letter of resignation, I commented, "I hope we know what we are doing." With that, Freda said, "I am doing this because you want to." Seems the brave hearts were failing at that moment and we laughingly blamed each other for this wild and foolish decision. Too late, the die was cast.

Imagine working your own hours, being able to take off when you want to, being at liberty to try new ideas, no boss looking over your shoulder, and best of all, making lots of money. Yep, that's a dream alright.

Actually, our dream wasn't quite that specific although we were brimming with great excitement at the idea of starting a business. One fact that pushed us along was that we owned land in Pennsylvania and one day expected to build a house there.

Freda's father had died suddenly, and her mother was living alone in McConnellsburg. Another decision to move to Pennsylvania was to help take care of her mom. I had been adopted into the Raker family, so it seemed the natural thing to do.

Lest you think we are completely foolhardy, let me explain that we are people of big faith and clearly trusted God for guidance in this decision. As an example, while all this was in the planning stages, our faith was so strong I wrote a song. Really, the plans were not much more than a big dream in 1971, but we were moving ahead with a plan for building a home in Pennsylvania. We referred to it as the Place. About this time, we were studying the story of Abraham at our Bible study. God told Abraham to pack up and move his family. God didn't tell him where to settle but said, "I have a place for you."

We weren't sure what was going to happen but knew God had a place for us. And so the song called simply "The Place" was written. We did then and continue to travel by faith.

The Place

Faith makes us certain of the things we do not see.
Faith tells us God has made a place for you and me,
For just like Abraham, who followed God's command,
Found God's place for him of rest and peace.
For God has made a place for us
Where we shall thrive, where we shall thrive.
Yes, God has made a place for us
Where we shall dwell in peace.
We shall run and not be weary.
We shall walk, but we'll not faint.
For the Lord himself dwells in us
He is our strength, our resting place.

Sing a new song now unto the Lord.
Sing His praise throughout the earth
For He will care for us,
Provide a place for us.
He is the Holy One, the Lord our God.

Looking back now, we see this song was prophetic. God certainly did find a place for us, where we have dwelled in peace and certainly did thrive. We walked through trials but did not faint. God was our source of wisdom and comfort and our rest. And surely we sing his praises every day.

Good-bye, New Jersey. Hello, Pennsylvania. No welcoming bands or parades awaited us and no specific job. My plan to teach school was not taking shape because no jobs were available. I had a new car, was building a new house, and I liked to eat. All great motivators to do something to bring in revenue.

The beginnings of businesses are probably as varied as there are businesses, but for us it started with a Christmas card.

While we were living in New Jersey, Freda designed a card for friends and family. Having an artistic and creative talent is a big plus when starting a gift business, and Freda took a big bow in that department. The Christmas card was painted by Freda, printed, and then sent out to family and friends. It was so well received with many compliments that the next idea flowed naturally. Why not do some social notes with scenes of local historical interest? Why not? Freda had designed four lovely social notes. The printer (a cousin, J. R. Miller, who owned his printing company) was available. The investment would be small, so why not give it a try? We had five hundred each of four scenes printed. That was the easy part. So now we had a total of two thousand note cards and envelopes in our hands, and now the challenge—how to market them.

A small digression: have you ever noticed how some people—maybe even yourself—who are gifted and/or creative, take pleasure in giving their creations? They love to give their work as gifts to friends and family, and the gifts are always enthusiastically received. Funny how items are so much more popular when given away than when they are being sold.

If you are anything like us, however, sell we must. And so the trial and error began. We were still in the hobby stage, and honestly, at that point, no one, including me, ever thought it would go much beyond that.

I wander here; let's get back to selling the note cards. Now the business "hat" has to be put on. Shall we sell two thousand singly or package them, ten to a package? Seemed to us it would be a lot less work selling two hundred packages rather than two thousand singly. And so we went for the package deal. Fortunately, those wonderful little sandwich bags were just the right size for ten notes and ten envelopes. We were off to production. We stapled a little header on the package printed with our name and number of notes in each package. Not real classy but looked good to us.

The first sales were easy because our friends in Salem County, New Jersey, were delighted with them and bought them both for gifts and personal use. Sound easy? We thought so too, and with that big success, we promptly ordered another printing of two thousand.

Now that we had saturated our friends and acquaintances with our product, we had to take the next step. It was here that we got a quick and valuable education on wholesale and retail. We were totally ignorant on this scene. So where to start?

I went to one of the nicest gift shops in the area armed with several packages and samples of our notes. I asked for the owner (whom I had never met). He appeared from somewhere while I was looking around and trying to look nonchalant. I didn't want to look too eager on my first try at selling. I soon found that this owner was not the most gracious or personable man. Actually, he was downright rude when it came to sharing the facts of business with me. My price to him and our suggested retail price made him laugh. He thrust the samples back at me and suggested that some women's organization should be selling them. I had to digest that reaction quickly and admit my ignorance at wholesale/retail pricing. This was my first try at selling the notes to a shop, and I had no idea what the expected markup was on an item or how the business worked. I mustered up all my charm, ventured another question, and got hit again. Although not particularly gentle or polite, this gentleman was quick to share some not-thought-about facts that I needed to know. "Do you have any idea how much it costs to keep a retail store open? Beyond paying a person to stand at the cash register, consider the rent, insurance, light, heat, advertising, etc. There is also the gamble of buying things that don't sell and have to be sold below cost. That is a real loss along with what may be stolen. Don't forget the interest payments that have to be made on the money borrowed to pay for goods to stock the store." He said, "Have I told you enough?" Wow, had he ever! I had enough to think about and incentive to look at the retailer's point of view.

I think the owner of the store must have realized he had hit me rather hard with his outburst and really did like the product. He and I came up with the idea of selling the notes singly where he could charge a little more and make his profit. Bottom line, before I left, he had bought eight dozen notes. Whew, I walked out a little nervous, happy for the sale, and a whole lot smarter. I really felt like quitting, but instead, I got into my car and went to two neighboring towns, selling to a shop in each town. In that short ride to the next town, I had raised the retail price to cover the retailer's profit margin. The next buyers never knew I had, just an hour earlier, learned the ways of the wholesale gift industry! A lesson I never forget.

CHAPTER 2

Accidental Education

Our hobby now was growing. New note cards with cats and seedpod designs added to the line. About that time, Freda had some interest in needlepoint and somehow got the idea to design needlepoint kits. Again, the design was easy, but where to buy materials like yarn, needlepoint canvas, needles, etc., all the things needed in a kit? Remember, this was long before the Internet, and finding materials, especially buying at wholesale prices, was a much bigger challenge than it is today. How to source resource material without Google? Well, since we knew no one in the business, we did the only thing we knew to do. We bought the kind of yarn we thought we would like and then wrote to the company for prices. Imagine our surprise when a salesman called and wanted to come and show us the line of yarns. Wow, where were we going to see him? In our home? Actually, we finally told the truth and explained we were new, just getting started, and needed prices. That was our first experience of finding a source.

More education. We were introduced to minimum orders, something we knew nothing about. We found that then a minimum order of yarn was usually $50–$100 and up. Somewhere, and I can't remember where, we heard about a gift show in Philadelphia. Since the show included a Sunday, we decided to go. What we did not know was that only established businesses were able to get into that wholesale show. Who knew?

I explained at the registration booth that we were just starting a business. After a lot of talk and persuasion from me, the lady at the registration finally allowed us to go into the show. Oh yes, we had to give the name of our business. What? I looked and Freda, and she looked at me, and on the spot, our business became the F and H Shoppe. *F* for Freda and *H* for Helen. Notice how sophisticated we were on the spot? The shop with the *pe* on the end?

In we went to our first gift show. It was a big learning experience. It was dazzling to us and filled our minds with lots of new ideas. We know now that the show was a small regional show, but in those days, it was a biggie for us.

Monday was back to work at our respective jobs, and the gift business was temporarily put to rest. Notice I said *temporarily*, because honestly, the gift business idea never really left our minds, but since we were not interested in quitting our jobs at that time, we needed a way to market our products other than an ordinary gift shop.

What would it be? Mail order. Sounded like a perfect situation. We could run a mail-order business and still work at our full-time jobs. The investigation into mail-order business will take a whole chapter in itself, so I'll just say we researched it thoroughly and decided to give it a try.

Let me skip over the details of printing two small catalogs. While we had good response from those two mailings, our plans took a different turn, and before we knew it, we were in a different type of gift business. Incidentally, we had no problem getting lovely handmade items for our catalogs. We had friends and friends' friends who had talent, ideas, and a product just ready to be sold.

That gift show in Philadelphia and the gift business kept calling us, and our ideas grew stronger. We visited other shows and talked to other people.

Take Every Opportunity to Market Your Product

To sum it all up in the simplest form, we learned the following lessons. Find a place to sell or market your product. That may be through craft fairs, retail stores, party plans, mail order, or whatever method you come up with. You must be prepared to price your items so the retailer will be able to have a 50 percent markup on it. If you are serious about your business, you need to purchase your materials wholesale. We used the old-fashioned method of writing or telephoning companies who made the kind of materials we needed and got prices. Today, of course, it's a whole new world, and with the touch of a button, you can be on the Internet and find hundreds of sources. Lucky you!

Oh yes, important! One of the first things you need to do is get a business card. Remember, as I've said before, there are many people who will help you find your way through the wholesale market. Don't underestimate the public library. We read lots of "how to" books from marketing, packaging, to financing and accounting. Remember, we did not have Internet, so the library was the best thing at that time.

Armed with that education, fast-forward a couple of years, new ideas, plans, and a giant leap forward. We did it! Our secure jobs, along with that monthly paycheck, ended, and our "business for yourself" started.

Now just in case you are reading this book and have an idea for a business tucked away in the back of your mind,

I hope you are thinking a bit bigger than before. Let me lead you to the next adventure from a hobby subsidized financially by our full-time employment to jumping into business with both feet or, should I say, all four feet for the two of us.

Sink or swim and maybe float a little.

CHAPTER 3

A Place to Live, Create, Design, and Share

And now for another giant leap of faith: building a home. Every weekend, we traveled from New Jersey to Pennsylvania to add a little more to this project. Once the foundation was dug, we had the frame of the house built. With our "we can do anything" attitude, we planned to finish the house ourselves. That meant putting in the insulation, nailing up drywall, finishing the drywall, measuring and cutting all the woodwork trim, and then, of course, the staining and painting. It was our good fortune that we were not brave enough or crazy enough to think we could do the plumbing or the electrical wiring. We had that contracted to professionals. At the end we discovered that some of what we had been sure we could accomplish, we could not. Sometimes, people we hired to do things had schedules not compatible to ours. But we went ahead, step-by-step. Often it seemed agonizingly slow, and at other times, we were excited at each visit to see our progress.

This place we were building would be where we would run the business. Plans were designed for a showroom. With this showroom in mind, we partitioned our 28' × 40' basement into three rooms. One for selling retail, a small one for packaging and shipping, and another fairly large room for a workroom. In November 1972, the Overly-Raker

Showroom was opened. We didn't have much fanfare about it. We put a small ad in the local paper, told a few friends we had met since moving here, and off we went.

Naturally, November is a good time to start a shop with the Christmas season upon us; however with us, it wasn't good preplanning. It was just the time we finally got the room and merchandise together. Some folks call it dumb luck.

We had our own designed and produced products. We also had other very carefully selected items. Freda and I spent a great deal of time looking for exceptionally good, handcrafted items that were different from the general run of things. Also we had several friends who put items in the shop on consignment. Most things were a one of a kind, all excellent quality. We appealed to the discriminating buyer. But we didn't have great crowds of buyers. Those who came generally did buy, and best of all, they brought other friends back with them.

As to this location (Place), we had neither traffic (maybe a car or two a day) nor population. This lovely rural community of approximately 1,400 people is McConnellsburg, Pennsylvania, which is the county seat of Fulton County, with the entire population of the county being approximately 15,000 people. I tell you this either so you'll have better sense than to start a shop "way out in the boonies" or to tell you that, if you have the right merchandise and give good, pleasant service, you can start a shop anywhere.

To keep you informed in the beginnings of this "journey," the initial idea to all this business was that only one of us would run the business full-time and the other would work to help support it. Freda, the artist, would paint and design new gift items and take care of the retail business, and I would continue teaching school. Like most of our original plans, that plan too took a different route. There were no teaching positions open. That door was closed. We had learned that when the Lord closes one door, he will open another. The hard part is to have faith and be patient until the next door is opened.

Keep tuned; you will see the doors that opened!

Location: Where to Start a Business

If you have read most of the how-to books on how to start a business, you find they spend some time on the location. Pick a high-traffic location. Do a traffic-flow survey etc. Choose a location near a large population. All this is excellent advice and certainly can make your job of building a business a much-easier task. Now remember all this good advice as I give you a mental picture of where we started our business. Actually, our first goal was a small mail-order catalog, so our location was not important. I say this in advance so you won't think we were completely without a plan or, worse yet, completely good-judgment-challenged.

Picture a small rural community. Yes, you can picture it, but that was not our location. Leave the town, and drive about five miles, three miles of hard surface road and a small bump onto a no-surface dirt road. On the last two miles of dirt road (mud when wet), you pass one mobile home and two farms. If you don't think that is not bad enough, suddenly the road narrows to little more than one lane. Now you are sure you must be lost and there cannot be a business here. Not so, don't give up, just another quarter mile, and you will have it. Well, almost... there is still a very pretty driveway up into the woods that takes you to our showroom. What a location! But that was the way it was.

CHAPTER 4

Overly-Raker Village: A Destination

Our place was where people could literally eat, drink, shop, and be merry. Within our first five years, that one room grew to two rooms in the basement plus two additional buildings outside and a tiny garden tearoom and the gallery on the main floor plus additional growth in the wholesale business. We didn't have a retail store. We had a retail village. We wanted our customers to have an experience when they visited us. Our cellar rooms were like a general store. It was here you could find everything from quilts, pillows, brass lamps, to wooden toys, handmade jewelry, and sculptures. Our antique cabinets, desks and tables were used for display. We even had a children's corner to keep them entertained while their parents shopped.

The barn was the home of our hand-thrown pottery, leather, and other goodies. Many of the pottery designs were done exclusively for us. We had artists who did special, made-to-order pieces for our customers. The leather items included belts, buckles, boxes, and hanging planters. Included in the barn were Freda's social notes of local historical interest. One of her specialties was personal Christmas cards she designed specifically for customers.

The Ivy House served as a temporary studio for Freda. Her handsome watercolor paintings were on exhibit there.

The garden tearoom was tiny but allowed customers to enjoy tea, coffee and cold drinks. At times, I could even be talked into entertaining customers with my music, mostly folk songs. The gallery was moved to its permanent home. It was actually the main floor of our home, but it housed Freda's artwork, both watercolors and sculptures.

We invited other local businesses into our village by collaborating with them to provide our customers with hay rides, buggy rides, sleigh rides, or horseback rides.

Our village was something special. We created memories as well as offered great products.

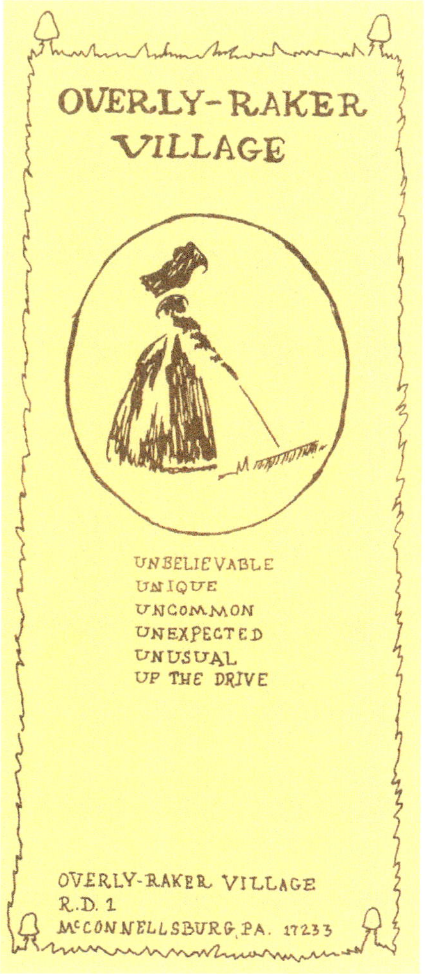

Demonstrations to Garden Clubs

Realies, the little product line that opened up a lot of doors for us!

We introduced the Realies into our retail and wholesale businesses as our first production item. As things happened, a lady from a prominent garden club in an adjoining town went to our retail shop and saw this little dried mushroom item. She was so fascinated. Her question, would we go to the garden club and demonstrate or discuss how we made these dried arrangements? (We were a fun, informative program for free). This, in turn, led their members to go to our shop and see all the other beautiful handmade things, and word spread, and so did our business.

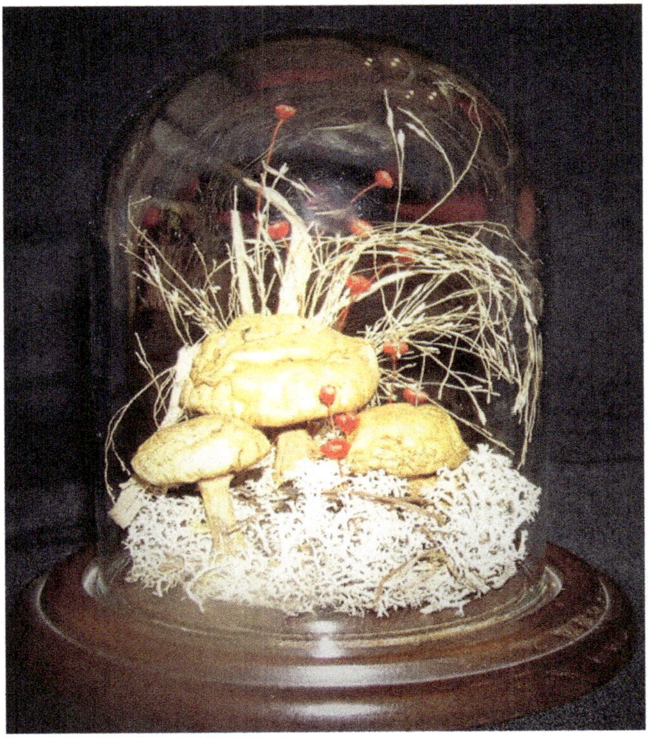

A Realie

When I mentioned we had one-of-a-kind handmade items, I need to explain that Freda and I searched for artists selling wholesale. We went to places like Bennington, Vermont, to a wholesale market, and other places where artists were just beginning their business and coming out with wonderful handmade items. That was in the early 1970s, when handmade things were just becoming popular. Not only did we have beautiful handmade pottery, leather handbags and belts, macramé hangings, tinware, and sterling silver jewelry, but our prices were better than those in the city with their high overhead.

Add to that Freda's beautiful watercolor paintings. We became a destination for special gifts and visits.

At about the same time we opened our little shop, small tracts of land, ten to twenty acres in size, were being developed in this and the surrounding counties. People from Washington, DC, and Baltimore, Maryland, were buying these land tracts for weekend residences.

Once some of these folks found us, they would take their guests who visited on the weekends, and we, yes, we, became a destination. In this rural area, there were not a lot of choices for a place to entertain folks on the weekends. We were it! Retail business flourished.

An added bonus for our customers was the very small sunroom with three little ice-cream tables and chairs (these were all we had room for). We offered free coffee or tea and had available a cookie jar with Dorie's famous homemade sugar cookies,10¢ each.

Dorie Fell, Freda's sister, was a registered nurse who, after the sudden death of her husband, moved from Massachusetts to be closer to us. She had three young boys and expected to continue nursing. However, she would help us that first summer until school started for the boys, and then she would go to work in the hospital. Our business was growing by leaps and bounds, and we needed a full-time person to oversee business, both retail and production. Dorie never went back to nursing except if we had someone cut a finger or needed their blood pressure checked. She became our right hand and invaluable to our business.

Back to the cookies. Dorie makes the best sugar cookies in the land. It was hard to visit our village and not have a cup of coffee and one or two of Dorie's cookies. Just another plus in making our Place a lovely place to visit.

CHAPTER 5

Chosen for Leadership: Fulton Fall Folk Festival

Along with our business experiences after moving into this small community, we became active in the Chamber of Commerce and other organizations. Since we were a tiny business, really in the embryonic stage, we felt that we should go to, or belong to, the Chamber of Commerce. It wasn't long after we became acquainted in the chamber that the president announced our county was the only county in Pennsylvania that did not have a tourist promotion agency. Somehow, even though we were quite new, I was asked to chair a committee to begin a tourist promotion agency. That gave me a thought.

Remember, I was a teacher, and although I did not get a full-time job as I had anticipated, I substituted a short time. My first day at substituting was the day before Christmas vacation. Surely you know that is a tough day even for full-time teachers. But here I was, ready to take on the high school students for a day. I was introduced to the principal, who gave me the schedule and incidentally gave me a warning about the third-period class: a class of juniors who were known to be rabble-rousers, surely a class that would give a new substitute a hard time.

I shall never forget it. It was my fashion to stand at the classroom door to greet the students. It also allowed me to see what was happening in the halls. The third-period students began to file in when my first and only challenge came swaggering up to me. "Question," he said, "are we going to have a party?" My immediate reply was "Did you bring the ice cream?" He was slightly unarmed for a second at my reply then quickly recovered. "No, but I can try and get some." I laughed and told him not to get me in trouble on my first day here.

We became immediate friends, and he announced to the class that I was "cool." Matter of fact, he stood up and told the class I was "a supercool lady." Not a bad reputation to have with the known leader of the pack. Thus, my first day was a success, along with subsequent days.

Interesting, as some of the high school students got to know me, they wanted to know why I would move here to the country. In their view, there was nothing here. As often is the case, young folks, and some old too, don't appreciate where they live and what is beautiful and wonderful about it, those things seen through the eyes of outsiders.

Tourist promotion? Here was our chance to tell a story of a lovely piece of extraordinary country, beautiful mountains, and quiet beauty.

Now back to the Chamber of Commerce story.

I, along with Harold Cullings, the then president of the chamber, and another member, Clyde Bookheimer, traveled to Harrisburg and the Commerce Department to talk about seed money for funding a new agency here. On the way back, we talked about what we would promote; we had beautiful mountains, hunting, fishing, lovely environment, but what new thing would we have to bring in tourists? I said we needed an event. It was decided we would get a committee together and promote an event. While traveling home, we brainstormed a bit, and I suggested that, since we were primarily agricultural here, perhaps we could have old farm days. Nothing was decided at that point. When I returned home, I got a select group together to brainstorm this new idea.

Remembering back, we met in our living room. Freda and I hosted the newly formed committee. Members were Betty Palmer, Anne Gobin, Clyde Bookheimer, Helen Bloomfield, Anne Lodge, Freda Raker, Jack Blattanberger, and Pat Decker. Here we hammered out an idea, both the idea, plus the date/time of the year and ideas for the few things we were going to do.

The date. We were careful to keep away from any other activities or festivals in the area so as not to compete with other functions in the county. The date was set for the third weekend in October and still remains that date after all these years.

The name: Fulton Fall Folk Festival. Personally, I was still set on that "old farm day's theme" and wanted to call it Fulton Fall *Farm* Folk Festival but was shot down, warned that no one would remember the long name or, worse yet, be able to say it! Hindsight, they were correct. Even yet, some of the people never call it by its correct name. I have heard it renamed when folks are talking about it as the Foliage Festival. That was never in the original, but I don't care what they call it, just so they come out and support it.

But now where to start. Being the chairperson, I took the lead in contacting people about this new tourist "happening." As always, there are skeptics with every new thing we attempt to do. So it became a sales job along with organizing what began as a small festival.

First we had to convince businesses to advertise in something they had never seen or heard of and honestly didn't get a picture of what it might materialize into. Guess what, I and some of our committee members weren't sure either, but we had a dream, we had a vision, and we thought we could pull it off. We were determined to have a parade. Keeping with our agricultural heritage, we had old farm tractors and equipment, an old restored steam engine, a couple of vintage cars, a farmer who literally rode an ox (well-trained) in the parade, a float from one of the banks, and some horses bringing up the rear of the parade. We had a high school band and a couple of businesses with a float to advertise their specialties. We dressed up in old period clothing to keep the flavor of the old farm days. I still laugh and say we had a fifteen-minute parade that we stretched into twenty minutes, but it was our first and we were proud of it. People on the street said, "Is that all there is?" Now, forty or so years later, the parade has grown so much that people on the street say, "Will this parade ever end?"

My dream was to have something happening in the whole county, not just one place, so every participant in the county could get a piece of the action and some of the revenue that tourism brings in.

Freda and I, who were with our little upstart business, took time out to travel to different parts of this small county, persuading people to have something going in their area for tourists. Remember, we hadn't had a festival before, so local people had no idea what to expect. Me neither! For the moment, it was just an idea with some advertising to come to this new Fulton County Festival, the third weekend in October. Maybe these two crazy ladies, fairly new to the area, might be on to something.

The southern end of our county had a successful sorority group who had a car show and a local arts and crafts show. The central part of the county had some craft shows. The businesses decorated with welcoming signs and specials for the weekend. The Greenhill Sewing Club had an apple butter boil (visitors were able to help stir the apple butter), where they made and sold apple butter and apple dumplings. That is still one of the popular events to visit each year. Churches made food, from the ever-popular chicken corn soup to all kinds of baked goods and apple dumplings, a fall specialty here. Some had ham or turkey dinners. The volunteers made lots of food. The Hustontown Fire Hall, northern Fulton County, had three days of serving many people. Great fund-raisers for lots of locals. Even with the restaurants and others making food, the first year, everyone sold out because of larger crowds than were expected.

A popular place to visit was the Burnt Cabins Grist Mill, still in working condition and grinding and selling stone-ground flour. They served buckwheat cakes and sausage. There was even a talent show there along with a contest to see who could eat the most pancakes.

How did we advertise? Remember, we had a grant from Pennsylvania Department of Commerce and our local county commissioners gave us some money, so we went all-out with advertising. Freda, being the artist, did some posters and designs for placemats that we had printed. We tried to sell the placemats to the restaurants (not many bought) but finally had to give them away.

TV! Yes, we surely did a TV ad in the local Altoona, Pennsylvania, and Hagerstown, Maryland, stations. I wrote a song and sang it. The song was illustrated with some great pictures to go along with it. The pictures were done by a local man then working in the art department of JLG Industries.

The song goes like this:

Let's go to the country; I mean Fulton County.
That's where it will happen in the fall.
Let's go to the country and bring all the family.
We'll have the best weekend of all.
October is the month; third weekend is the time.
We'll have lots of things to do, something for you and you.
Apple butter boil and a muzzleloader meet
Old farm equipment and buckwheat cakes to eat.
We'll have tours of houses and country music.
Craftsmen will be there in that good ole country air.
Let's go to the country; I mean Fulton County.
That's where it will happen in the fall!

That is a long story to tell you of the beginnings of something that has grown to be the biggest thing that happens in this county every year. It has taken on a life of its own and is now quite different from when we started, but it is tourism at its best! I have been credited with starting it, but there were, and are, lots of people who made it successful.

As part of the festival in 1975, I gave a commemorative plate to President Ford. To my delight, he wrote me back.

THE WHITE HOUSE

WASHINGTON

February 5, 1975

Members of the Fulton County
Chamber of Commerce:

I want to thank you for the commemorative plate in honor of the 1974 Fulton Fall Folk Festival which you so kindly gave to Dr. James Connor for me.

As we approach the Bicentennial, it is indeed heartening to see the people of our country take a new interest in their local and national history. By knowing where we come from, we will better know where we are going.

Your gift reflects the rich agrarian heritage of your community and will serve as a lasting reminder of your friendship.

With warm best wishes.

Sincerely,

The Fulton County Chamber
of Commerce
McConnellsburg
Pennsylvania 17212

Was it easy? Nothing worthwhile is often easy. But if you are called to do something good, do it. Yes, there was, will be, criticism, mostly from those who do nothing. But stay strong.

A perfect example is our second festival, when we had a very rainy weekend. Friday night, people got stuck in the mud at the gristmill, and the next morning, I received calls from people grumbling at our poor choice at having part of the event there. Along with that, it was raining, literally on our parade. What to do? Have the parade or cancel and on and on. It was such a dark, dismal day. I got rather depressed at all the hits coming at me. But as I looked out into the woods at the rain and wind, I looked at all the trees blowing and swaying. I noticed how the taller trees were bending the most. The thought came to me, *Tall trees catch much wind.* Where that thought came from, I really don't know, but it said to me, if you are going to be a tall tree (leader), you will catch the negative wind as well as the positive. That thought suddenly turned my attitude around. Did the rain stop? No, but it stopped in my mind, and off we went to a successful, damp weekend.

And by the way, I think we have successfully taught the young folks here that we/they have lots to be proud of. Hundreds of people come back every year to see us, envious of this place. Proof that, while we are small and rural, we are blessed with a wonderful area.

Below is a quote from Donna Gordon, who was from the Penn State Fulton County Agriculture and Home Economics' extension office.

> Early in the late 1960's tourist promotion was on the meeting agenda at the Fulton County Agriculture and Home Economics' Extension office. Mr. H. P. Kies was County Agent and I, Donna Gordon,

was Home Economist. The topic of discussion was on how Fulton County could develop tourism. A committee was formed and met with the Chamber of Commerce, who was already working on ways to promote Fulton County.

Mr. Kies had met a newcomer to our county, who spoke favorably about the beauty we have here and how it could be shared. Her name was Helen Overly. She got his attention and he suggested that we invite her to share her excitement at a joint meeting with the Chamber of Commerce. Some of the thoughts and ideas from that meeting were: People will come. We have much to offer. The beauty is here. We need to locate talented people who do painting, woodworking, quilting, crafts, etc. My favorite was, get them to come to Fulton County and leave their money here!! I remember talking about fall being a beautiful time of year and having an event during the third week in October and calling it Fulton Fall Folk Festival (FFFF). Some of the early events and activities of the FFFF was an Old Timer's Parade, Green Hill Sewing Club Apple Butter Boil, Southern Fulton Arts and Craft Show sponsored by the Sorority, Fulton County Extension Homemaker's Quilt Club Show, sewing historical costumes, and window displays of costumes and antiques.

Much honor goes to Helen Overly for believing in her dream and being here to see it fulfilled.

The success of that festival was somehow a reason for me being selected for the chamber's prestigious Man of the Year award. Remember, this was the early seventies, when women were not often popular in leadership roles. As it was said, it was still the "good ole boys'" world, especially in the rural areas.

At the chamber's awards ceremony, Loy Garber, a young minister in the community, gave this presentation:

> Helen Irene Overly
>
> Well... it was bound to happen! Male Chauvinism just couldn't go on forever!
>
> Here in the 20th century... man is beginning to painfully admit the truth about the Garden of Eden. The Good Lord... in all His wisdom... put someone else in that Garden and that someone else was a woman. This was not to be solely a man's world. No indeed! Instead... this was to be a place where both men and women could equally share this world's milk and honey.
>
> So times are a changing! And it's about time too! All over the world, more women are playing a decisive and important role in shaping the destiny of the planet. So much so... that 1975 has been declared by many nations as the International Year of Women.
>
> And therefore it is most appropriate that this year's Fulton County Chamber of Commerce "Man of the Year Award" be changed to the Woman of the Year.
>
> So to all past recipients of the Man of the Year Award... please move over and make room in your fraternity for a well deserving society sister. For tonight history is being made in Fulton County... as HELEN IRENE OVERLY becomes 1975 Women of the Year... for her outstanding service to our community.

I would like to take a few moments to share with you, some incidents of the life of Helen Overly, just so you may gain an appreciation for why she is so deserving of this Award.

Many years ago (I have been sworn to secrecy as to just how many) in the Western Pennsylvania village of Wyano, a baby girl was born into the family of Edgar and Clara Overly. Helen Irene was to become one of seven children.

As she grew older, Helen received her secondary education in the Greensburg School System. And it was here that she discovered she could sing, and sing well! It's true that at first her knowledge of the musical field was somewhat limited. But with encouragement of her high school music teacher her musical talents and knowledge were developed. And developed quite successful for in both her junior and senior year Helen was chosen to represent her school at the state Chorus. An honor reserved for only a select few of talented students throughout the Commonwealth.

And Helen has been carrying a song in her heart ever since.

Singing has become one of her beautiful ways of communicating thought and ideas to the people she meets. In the past she had her own radio show on Station WJIC in New Jersey. And in the present you may have the privilege of tuning in her singing every Thursday at 1:15 PM on WCHA or you might be fortunate enough to see her perform at many local banquets and social events.

After high school it was on to South Carolina and further educational pursuits at Bob Jones University. But unfortunately Helen was forced to terminate her college education for economic reasons.

So on to Wilmington, Delaware she went. There she found a job as the manager of the Montgomery Ward Catalogue Store. It didn't take Helen long to make her presence felt. With her own ingenuity she devised all kinds of unheard of sales gimmicks and techniques, soon her Store had the most outstanding sales record in all of Delaware, Eastern Maryland and South Jersey.

When I was interviewing her for this award, I asked her: "How did you do it?" She chuckled and said, "I guess I was just plain gutsy, that's how I did it."

I believe "gutsy" in the best sense of that word, says a lot about how Helen was to achieve many of the things in her life.

For example, the Wilmington Trust Company advertised for a new Assistant Personnel Director. MUST be a college graduate. But Helen with only two years of college applied for the job anyway and, yes, got the job. For eight years she served as the director of some 12 hundred personnel in that big city Trust Company.

After 12 years of working in the Wilmington area Helen returned to college at Glassboro State University to work hard to receive a degree in Elementary Education.

Then it was to the Penns Grove School District in New Jersey to teach for six years.

It was during her years in Wilmington that Helen met a very talented lady by the name of Freda Raker.

While in the Wilmington area she and her new friend Freda led the parade to build a church. Faith in her Creator is a very important motivating force in Helen's life style. She found many others in Newark, where she was living, who also shared her beliefs. They started worshiping in one another's home. As the group of believers grew larger it became evident that a church building was needed. Since the cost of contracting someone to build a church edifice was financially out of reach, Helen comes up with a brilliant idea: we will build our own church building. And so she was off and running on another new adventure.

Under her direction land was purchased, money raised, materials bought and the members were organized into work crews. All volunteers. One and half years later the building was completed at a cost of $35,000 and it was totally paid for. Now that is some kind of an accomplishment when you stop to think about it. Let's see, it took God a few thousand years to build His church and it still isn't paid for.

One of her favorite hobbies has been crafts and antiques. She decided to turn her avocation into a vocation. Teamed up with the fine artistry talents of Freda Raker, Helen and Freda came to Fulton County to undertake the business of running a quaint gift shop.

Then one day while walking in the woods near their shop, Helen noticed a few mushrooms. To her, there was something striking about their beauty. Freda did beautiful watercolors of flowers from the woods so why not a mushroom. Some of the mushrooms dried on Freda's drawing table.

Instead of throwing them away it was decided to mount the mushrooms on a board and hang it on the wall in gift the shop.

Well, visitors to the shop commented so favorably about the dried mushroom arrangement that Helen and Freda decided to go into the mass producing of decorative mushrooms. So during your travels if you have a moment to browse around a gift shop or two you just might discover a dried mushroom arrangement from Overly and Raker from Fulton County.

And this brings us to what I consider to be the prime reason why Helen Overly is so deserving of the Women of the Year award.

Just like she took a simple mushroom, helped everyone to see its worth and beauty, she has worked tirelessly during the past year to take the simplicity of Fulton County's historical heritage and make it so worthwhile and so beautiful in the eyes of the beholder.

As the Program Chairman of the Fulton County Historical Society, as President of the Fulton County Tourist Promotion Agency and, the energetic chairman of the very successful Fulton Fall Folk Festival committee, Helen has taken many of our fondest past memories of good old county-living and brought them back to life again. Helen has inspired us to:

- To put on our old frontier dresses and buckskin pants
- To heat up our apple butter copper kettles
- To prime our muskets

- To restore our historical homes and buildings
- To rediscover good old fashion eating of buckwheat cakes

Helen Overly has helped all of Fulton Countians to re-appreciate the simple things of their past heritage. Through her creative genius, the annual Fulton Fall Folk Festival will help Fulton Countians to enjoy the simple beauty of the good-old-days as they are relived time and time again. But more than that she has helped rekindle a pride within all of us.

Why has Helen Overly been at the forefront of so many challenging undertakings ever since she left home? I would venture to say that Helen has been a very self-reliant, independent, "gutsy" person, who from a young age learned how to stand on her own two feet and make her mark in the world. And what a truly outstanding mark she has made.

This was quite a tribute. As we were new to the community, this was our first time to this awards banquet, and I really didn't know how to respond to the presentation. I was not aware that I was to make remarks. Add to that, even more surprising, I was presented with a congratulatory letter from then-president Gerald Ford. I was so shaken by all this that all I was able to say was "Thank you."

You must be wondering how I have that whole presentation. This is how it happened! Loy and I volunteered on a scholarship committee together. At one of our meetings, he mentioned to me that, in cleaning out old files, he came across his handwritten notes from 1974.

He thought I might like to have them. Now these years later, we all have them.

CHAPTER 6

The Genesis of a "Realie"

Back to our new product: the Realies, a lovely, terrarium-like decorative piece made with a base of moss, dried mushrooms, with a touch of color or dried weeds from the woods. Then put on a wooden base under a glass dome and voilà! There you have it!

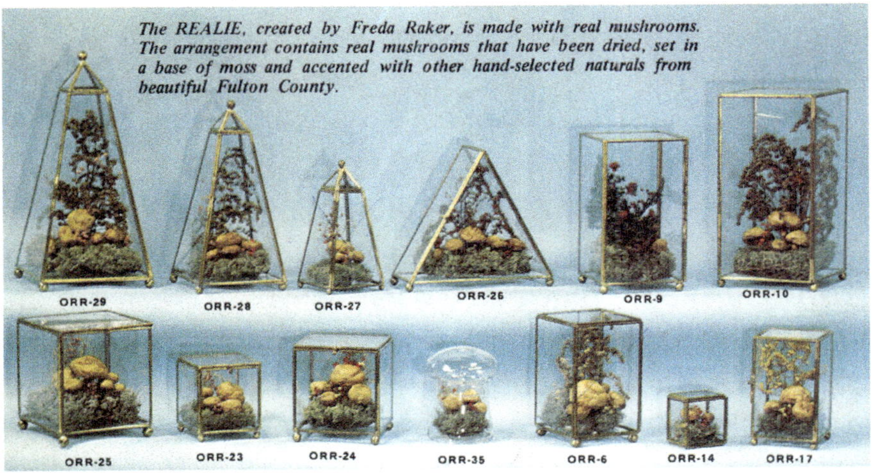

The mushrooms were dried and preserved, set in a base of reindeer moss from the woods with other hand-selected, natural forest products. The arrangements came in a variety of shapes and sizes, ranging from pictures framed in barn wood frames to large elegant glass and brass cases. There were also many arrangements made inside specially made wooden hanging-like lanterns inside ceramic eggs and even tiny arrangements made in cookie cutters to hang on the Christmas trees.

Wouldn't you say that God has a sense of humor? We needed to find a way to make money, and he gave us mushrooms and weeds from the woods. It was a great idea. So great we signed up for the four-day Philadelphia Gift Show.

Let's back up a bit to before the Realie creations were ready for mass production. It happened like this: Freda loved walking in the woods and enjoyed finding bits of nature that she could use in painting small watercolor pictures. Among her favorites were purple thistles, red and orange mushrooms, and Queen Anne's lace. One day, one of the mushrooms she had found in the woods dried on her drawing table. I remember she said, "I could mount this on a piece of watercolor paper and make it three-dimensional." With that, she painted some green grass then some blue in the sky, glued on the mushroom, and mounted the whole thing on a beveled wood piece for a wall hanging. I like to add that I put on the brass hanger.

Sometime later, visiting the beach, we picked up some driftwood pieces that made a perfect base for moss and small mushrooms to enhance the Realie creations. At the time, we were doing this just for fun and to give as gifts to our friends. But in due course, friends were asking to buy them to give as gifts. "So clever, so unique!" Music to our ears. All this was happening before we moved to Pennsylvania.

Drying a mushroom is a challenge. We were drying mushrooms before the day of food dehydrators. Therefore, we had to be creative because we had a problem. We had a product that demanded dried mushrooms. We tried a lot of things. Just laying the mushrooms out to air-dry was not going to be quick enough.

As the dried-mushroom business developed and grew, we needed a way to dry hundreds of mushrooms. How?

Freda and I put our engineering hats on. This was probably Freda's brainstorm. We got a big carton, and I made wire screens to fit the carton, kind of square screens, then used tin cans to set and separate the screens. We layered the screens, each set in place with more cans. Mushrooms were placed evenly on each screen. Our thought was that we needed warm air flowing through the screens that held mushrooms. Now, how to get that? This would probably be obvious to any woman: it's called a hair dryer. We cut a hole in the bottom of the box/carton and put a hair dryer in there, turned it on, and let it run 24-7 or until it burned itself out. Did it work? Oh my, yes! So much so that we built two more air/hair dryers to keep up with the demand for our dried mushrooms to make our Realie arrangements. We often had our own little private jokes when someone would go into our booth at trade shows and ask how we dried the mushrooms. I would say we air-dried them, and Freda would say later, "Did you say air-dry or hair-dry?"

Dorie, Freda's sister, scoured the yard sales, looking for cheap hair dryers. It is always nice to have a scavenger in the family.

When we say our business mushroomed, we weren't kidding. With the success of the first two trade shows and the popularity of our Realies, it was evident we needed more space and some help to make them. From our little space here in our house, we moved down to Freda's mother's basement for Realies production. It was a large 30' × 60' space, which gave us the space to add raw materials along with the people to make the product. In one weekend we built shelves, added a table or two, found some benches or chairs to sit on, and set up an assembly line for making our very special, real dried-mushroom arrangements.

The dried mushrooms, foliage, moss, and flowers were artfully arranged and placed in different containers. There were large and small domes on a wooden base along with glass and brass cases in multiple sizes. Originally, we gathered our own mushrooms out in the woods and gathered all the reindeer moss. But things were getting out of hand. Freda woke up one day in a panic, worried about what if it snowed and we couldn't go outside and pick more moss.

That presented the next challenge. Where do we buy the kind of moss that we needed and in what quantity? That was the beginning of buying moss. We bought mushrooms from the local grocery store, nine pounds at a time, every week, but we knew that there soon would not be enough and the price was too high. So we went to the "mushroom capital," which is Avondale, Pennsylvania, and begun to buy large quantities at a time. The grower took the mushrooms to a distribution place in Harrisburg, and we would go there and pick them up.

Harrisburg was about an hour's drive from ours. Not only did we have trouble finding and getting mushrooms and moss, but we also had problems finding large numbers of the glass and brass containers we needed.

At one of our early tradeshows in Chicago, we met Mr. Jacaman, who was a distributor of both tin items and glass and brass cases from Mexico. He saw our product and suggested that we could buy the glass and brass items from him. When buying larger quantities, the price was substantially lower, and it seemed like a good decision for us to order from him. With that in mind, we ordered the quantities that we needed for the present and projected what we would need later. That was the good news.

The bad news is the shipment did not come into Texas from Mexico on the date that he had anticipated and promised them to us. The shipment finally came in the first week in December. By this time, all our production was done and had been shipped to our customers. Here we were with a large quantity of containers that had to be stored and had to be paid for. That's just one of the problems that we faced in this little new, fledgling business.

If you have a problem, don't give up. There is usually a solution; you just have to keep trying to find it.

Enter Leon Hurst

Our business continued to grow and, with it, the need for more personnel with experience in certain areas.

Wouldn't you know in late 1979 we received a call from a friend who lived in West Virginia.

After pleasantries, he commented that he had been watching our little company grow and would be interested in being a part of it if we ever had a need. Oh my, yes, we had a need! Enter Leon Hurst, who certainly had the experience we needed, but how would be able to afford a person with his background and who was a family man too?

Well, God is always on time and never a minute too late! Surprise? We could hire him maybe part-time, three days a week, but that was a crazy idea. Hold on—believe it or not, that could work. Really? Leon had been working for a company that was downsizing, and he negotiated part-time work for them also. Perfect! Leon moved his wife, Sue, and his then-small son, Aubrey, to our area in 1980.

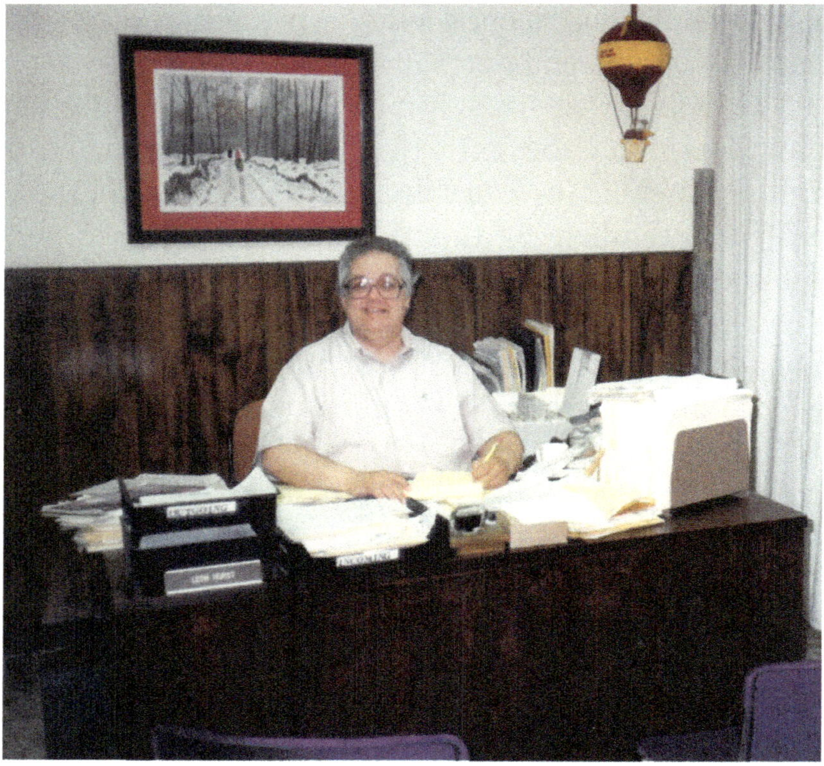

Leon Hurst

And what did Leon bring to the company? A much-needed inventory-control system and, best yet, his special purchasing talent. This was before Google. No matter what we needed purchased, Leon was able to find it. Both of these things were badly needed as Freda and I were struggling to fill all the duties demanded with the company's increasing growth!

Leon's part-time status lasted only about a month with us. We were moving to larger quarters, more work came in, and with him here, we had the staff to support it! Leon turned out to be an "all-purpose" talent! He was very creative and became the lead person to oversee all the advance setups for the gift shows. This, along with overseeing the operations at Overly-Raker. He had a great sense of humor. He had spent some time working for the Playtex Company and used to say he went from working with "girdles and bras to mushrooms and dolls."

Never let it be said that we were all work and no play. Overly-Raker had great Christmas parties and summer parties at our home, where we had employees and all their families. Leon was always on board to help us plan something extraspecial.

In 1992, Leon became vice president of operations for Overly-Raker Inc. What a blessing he was to our organization.

CHAPTER 7

The Tradeshow Way Realies Were a Hit!

At that time, we had lots of startup ideas, among them a gift catalog of handmade items that we and our friends were making. It included items from friends. Some of the things featured were lovely woven placemats, wooden toys, wooden trays, needlepoint kits, leather belts, wallets, and many other items. Of course, Freda's artwork was a most popular feature. I also somehow, edged myself into the manufacturing end, and cut wood plaques with our electric saw, sanded them smooth, and used decoupage for creating wall decor, with western and historical prints as a subject.

We did all the layout for the catalog and all the photography. In keeping with the theme of this catalog, we had it printed in sepia. Freda planned and executed the cover. But to our chagrin, the gift catalog we created was not quite as successful as we had expected. The big error was that we did not print or mail a large-enough number of catalogs. Another lesson learned.

The simple plan we had laid out was quickly unraveling. As weeks went by and September got closer, it was evident I was not going to get a teaching job in this new community. We both had enough common sense to know that we would not be able to pay the mortgage, make the car payments, and eat on what that first catalog (mailing of 3,500) and the small showroom sales would bring.

We often laughed and said if we sold everything we had, including inventory, we wouldn't have had enough to live on for more than a few months.

It quickly became apparent that we needed more sales than we could generate in our limited population based here in Fulton County. How to get a wider market?

Remember, we had learned about the Philadelphia Gift Show while still living in New Jersey. We had the name of the management company, the Little Brothers Show Management Company. So off went a letter to them inquiring about obtaining a space for our company as an exhibitor.

A letter soon arrived back from the office of the Little Brothers Show Management Company, with facts and figures regarding the show, along with an application. After mailing information back and forth, signing a contract, and sending a deposit, we were on our way to our second venture, moving into the wholesale market via a trade show.

Overly-Raker, the name we finally decided upon for our company, was listed in the Philadelphia Gift Show directory. We arrived in Philly in April 1973 with a very small gift selection but lots of duplicates. Our line consisted of social notes (selection of twelve designs), needlepoint kits (four designs), miniature hand-painted watercolors (selection of four), and our newest creation, the Realies! Real dried-mushroom arrangements.

We arrived at the hotel address, not knowing where to park or where to unload our exhibit and samples. Wouldn't you know the Lord had our helper waiting? We pulled up in back of a van loaded with what looked like display props to set up an exhibit. Sure enough, Ralph, a little Italian man, obviously a veteran in doing tradeshows, came back and introduced himself. Then he proceeded to give us directions on how to get into the exhibit area. He was the nicest man, and we were so grateful to meet him.

Now we were in. We set up our first show. In order to make the exhibit as attractive as possible, we arranged and rearranged nearly the whole day until we were satisfied. We were ready for the show opening on Sunday morning. Oh yes, and we were more than a little impressed with our name, Overly-Raker, and a small advertisement printed in the show directory. At last, we were in the big-time. I say that with tongue in cheek.

The gift show opened at 10:00 AM, and we saw people walk by our booth without stopping. This made us a bit uneasy since we were new and had invested a fair amount of money to participate in this show. However, at about noon, two ladies from Malvern, Pennsylvania, came in and looked at our product. They thought our items were wonderful, and they gave us our first order. The name of the company was the Brass Lantern. I will never forget it. We took many orders during that first tradeshow and knew that, for us, the show was highly successful. We were just ecstatic thinking people appreciated our product. It wasn't until we were on the way home that we realized what a job we had waiting for us at home. We had no inventory at home to fulfill these orders.

As soon as we got back to our office (better known as the basement), we took an inventory of raw materials we would need.

Speaking of office, we finally had to bite the bullet and hire someone to help in the office. Early on, we did everything: bookkeeping, secretarial stuff, etc. But now we were away at trade shows and needed someone to keep the office open. If you are new in business, keep your eyes open for good staff, especially for the office.

While I was out doing some volunteer work (starting a tourist promotion agency), I was "loaned" a person working for the county for some secretarial help. This person so impressed me because, when I gave her work, nearly before I got back to my business, she would phone to say it was done! We needed a person like that to help us; yes, we did.

We were so blessed. I called Linda Fix to come talk with us about a job and she said *yes*! We were still operating in the basement, not much of a sophisticated environment, but Linda, like the rest of us, was intrigued with this little business, all of us jumping through hoops to meet the demands of the next challenge. We were so small it was a "family affair," each helping the other to find success to the ongoing growth problems.

As we grew to a sizable business, anyone who knew me heard me bragging about Linda. She was my right and left hand, always on top of things and making sure I was in the right place at the right time, had all my assigned business commitments done on time, etc. A perfect administrative assistant. So perfect she became vice president of business administration, responsible for management of the business operations. We should all have a Linda!

With Linda in the office, Freda and I worked frantically to find all the items we needed to create the Realies and rushed to ship out the product to our new customers. That meant counting up all the orders, determining how many glass domes and how many glass and brass cases we needed to buy, and finding and drying the mushrooms. After counting what we needed to complete the orders, we took off for Williamsburg, Virginia, to buy the glass domes and glass and brass cases.

We were able to buy wholesale at the Williamsburg Pottery at that time. I gave the man at the wholesale section a list of what we needed to manufacture the Realies. In the meantime, Freda and I looked around at possible items we might be able to use. When we got back to the wholesale section, we saw cartons piled high at both sides of the door. Since there was no one else around, I asked the man working there, “Those are not all ours, are they?” But yes, they were. I backed our car into the pickup area. Seeing this, the man looked at me and said, “You don’t expect to get all these in there, do you?”

Well, yes, we got it all home, but we had to repackage things, take the glass domes and other glassware out of cartons, and repack them around the spare tire and in every nook and cranny of the trunk and backseat. Driving home, I never saw Freda, who was sitting on the passenger side. There was too much stuff stacked on the space between us. I could hear her over there, but the stacks of materials were too high for me to see her.

We had then, and continued to have, a “no problem” attitude. It was with this type of confidence, mixed with determination and a whole lot of faith, that we began our journey of creating a successful business venture.

Now the next problem. We definitely needed help but were not sure we would be able to afford to hire someone. Freda’s sister Babs and a cousin, Margie, were both interested in working for us. Both were talented in putting these things together artistically and would be willing to work three days a week. That schedule suited us fine. What I worried about was meeting a payroll, which we had not done before. That’s a scary situation. To add to my worry, the first thing I knew, Margie went out and bought a new car. Suddenly I thought, *Oh no, now we have to pay for that car*. Mother instinct, I guess, I felt obligated to provide them with work. But there was no problem. We had plenty of work and were able to pay them each payday. Orders kept coming to the point that at one time we had twelve ladies working making Overly-Raker Realies. It is hard to imagine now how we did it, but around that time, we established and built up the Overly-Raker Village too.

CHAPTER 8

The Philadelphia Friendship

We met the nicest people in the gift industry. The surprise was that everyone was so kind and supportive of one another, since we were all vying for the same customer base to sell our products, yet it wasn't a cutthroat business. We all admired one another's product and business.

At our first show in Philadelphia, we were just across the hall from a company called House of Davian. I need to insert here: that first show was held at the Ben Franklin Hotel, which had dedicated three entire floors with rooms for exhibiting gifts. Each exhibitor could choose to have the bed removed from the room, or some folks left the bed in the room and incorporated it around their display. I may add that some folks even slept in the room with their display. Worked out well because there was a bath and shower etc. and it saved paying for another room rate for the week. We were not one of those people. We had the bed removed and built a beautiful display.

Now back to our neighbor across the hall. The person in charge of that booth was a little Jewish man who had a fairly strong accent and had with him a young woman (his niece from Israel) who spoke no English at all. It turned out he was a manufacturer of fine silver jewelry and his name was Tzvi Wachtel. I well remember telling Freda that we should not get too friendly with him because he would be trying to sell us something. Already I pegged him as a high-pressure salesperson. I say that with a smile now because that man and his family became some of our very best friends. How did we really get to meet him?

At the end of our first day of that show, we were so excited because we had written some orders and we had friends from Delaware come to see the show. It was a novel experience for all of us. In our excitement as we left the show that night, we closed the door but left some handmade leather belts on the outside. (These were handmade belts that we were selling for someone else.) The next morning when we went to the show, this dear man, whom I wasn't going to get to acquainted with, came over with these belts and said, "You left these on the outside of the door last night, and I was afraid somebody would steal them, so I took them down for you."

That was the beginning of a friendship. To our surprise and delight, when we went to our first show in Chicago, who was across the aisle from us in that exhibit area but House of Davian. However, at this show our friend, Tzvi, was not present, but instead, his wife, Marcella, was there. As friendly as Tzvi was, Marcella was the opposite. She was very busy getting the display set up. We introduced ourselves, but no chitter-chatter with her. The show began, customers came and went, days went by, but it was not until Marcella's son, David, arrived at the show that we got acquainted.

David was about seventeen years old and had just traveled in from Israel, where he had spent the summer in a kibbutz. David was full of stories and songs and dance. As the gift show was winding down and fewer and fewer customers went in, David entertained us with Israeli song and dance. What a good time we had. To top it off, the new musical, *Grease*, was playing for the first time in Chicago.

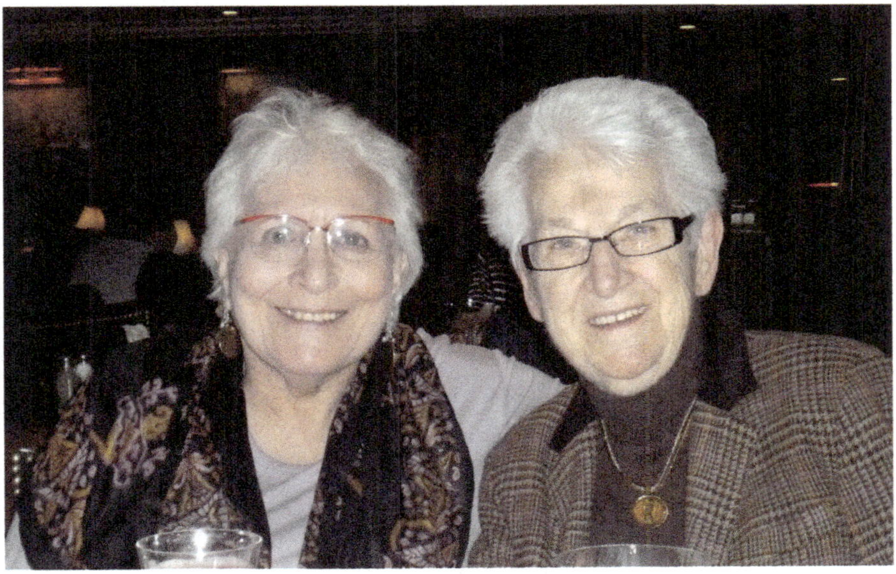

My friend Marcella Wachtel

CHAPTER 9

Chicago—First Time Exhibiting in the Windy City

While we were exhibiting in a very small show in Atlantic City (our second ever show after Philadelphia), some of the other vendors suggested we go to the Chicago Show. That was a big-time show. We had never even visited Chicago, so why not? Well, the catch was there was a wait list to get into that popular show. But often, things and circumstances happen to put you in the right place at the right time.

At breakfast at the hotel in Atlantic City, we overheard the people at the next table talking about their home in Danbury, Connecticut, and their place in White Plains, New York. I remarked to Freda that those people "must have money" because they had two homes. What I did not know was that they were Mr. and Mrs. Bill Little, owners of the trade show company, at that time, known as the Little Brothers Company.

Freda and I left the restaurant, which opened onto the boardwalk. There was a fierce gale blowing. Picture this! It was the year palazzo pants were totally trendy. If you have never seen them (they were not stylish for very long), they were long pants with huge, wide legs. Freda had made me a pair in bright red. Now here I am with pants that looked like red sails in this wind. Who should notice me as they looked out the restaurant window? Yep, Mr. Little and his wife.

Later in the day, this fine-looking gentleman came to our booth and admired our display. Then he commented to me, "I thought we were going to lose you in the wind this morning." That was our introduction to the man, Mr. Little, who was the manager of the Chicago Gift Show. This was the show that we would try to get into even though it might take one to two years to get a space.

I went to the Atlantic City show office to request a space in the Chicago Show. Later, near the last day of the show, Mr. Little's son, Will, came to our booth and said, "My father has a place in the Chicago Gift Show for you if you would like it." *Wow*. We said yes and were left to wonder how we were so lucky. Turned out two things had made a difference. One, we had a great eye-catching display with red, white, and blue, and two, who could forget the lady in red palazzo pants blowing down the boardwalk? Top that with the fact that Mr. Little liked red! We didn't know it at that time, but we had made an important friend.

The Chicago Gift Show encompassed three locations. The big, major companies were in the McCormick Place Exhibit area. Then the newer, smaller companies were housed at either the McCormick Hotel, which had a small exhibit hall, or the Palmer House, which had four rather small exhibit floors. We were placed at the Palmer House, right downtown in a pretty ritzy hotel, ritzy enough that the doorman dressed in top hat and tails.

Two months after the Atlantic City show, we were off to Chicago. We drove there with all our show samples packed in our LTD Ford. We arrived at the hotel, downtown on Monroe Street, at high noon, when the street was filled with city workers out to lunch. I was driving and pulled in behind a limo. In those days, limousines were not as common as they are now, and I felt a bit out of my league when I saw the doorman. I looked at Freda and said, "I can't get out here." She said, "Sure you can!" I did; she didn't. I explained to the doorman that we were here for the gift show. He quickly agreed to help us unload.

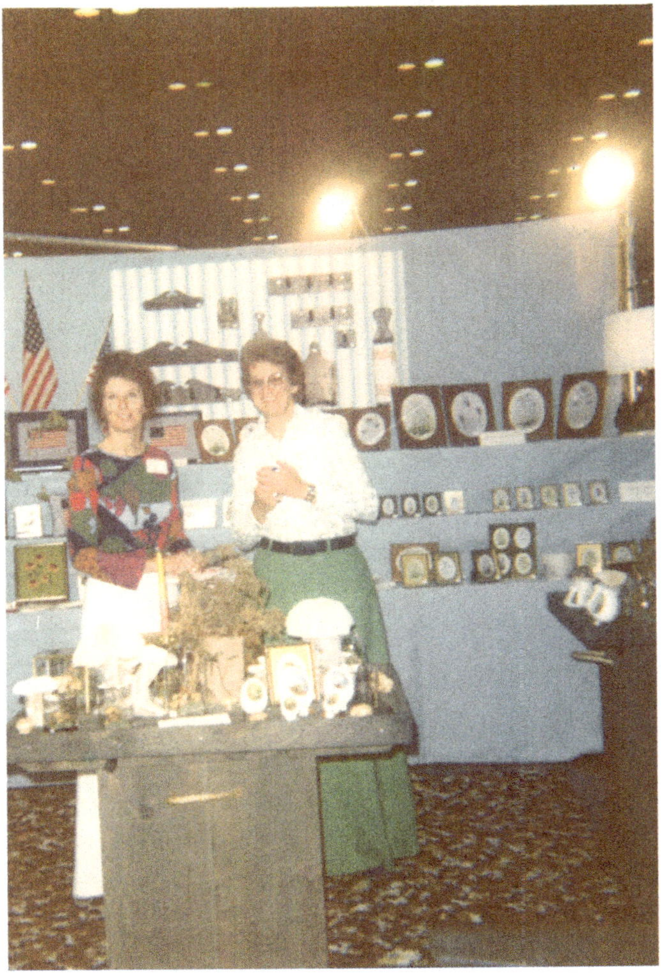

Early beginnings at a gift show

Oh my, we had all kinds of cartons with our product and display packed in the backseat and the trunk of the vehicle. The doorman quickly helped unload our things and set them on the street along the curb. Picture this, two pieces of nice luggage (those were our personal bags) and then five old pieces of luggage that our dear friend and neighbor, Lil Fithian, bought at auction for $5, not each, but all of them. Add to that cartons from the grocery store—Cheerios boxes, Pampers boxes, soup boxes—all with their own undisguised supermarket labels. The doorman told me I would have to go to park the car and told Freda she would have to stay there and watch what we had just unloaded. I laughed later and said, "Who would want that stuff anyway?" Sure didn't look very valuable to the average Chicagoan strolling on the street.

Me, go park the car in downtown Chicago? Without Freda, who was the chief navigator? Scary. Wasn't sure I would ever find my way back. But yes, I did.

Now came the process of lugging all that stuff to the exhibit floor, a difficult chore, even with the help of the bellman.

What an exciting surprise confronted us when we got to our assigned exhibit booth! We had been given a beautiful spot on the corner at the entrance, where buyers would see us on the way in and on the way out.

This was the beginning of the chapter that took us from that little 10' × 10' booth to the spacious 400 square feet of exhibit space twenty years later and, by the way, to the presidency of the Chicago Gift Show. I became the first women president of that show.

CHAPTER 10

The Road to Chicago via an Encouraging Word

Chicago's first show in that small 10' × 10' booth was good, but when we considered the expense for traveling, for renting a hotel room, for parking, and the expense of the show itself, we decided it was not financially wise to return to the second show. That decision was made. The contract for the next show came into our office. We thought we should write a letter, thanking the show management for the space but informing them we had made the decision not to renew the contract.

We thought that was the end of it, until we got a letter from Mr. Bill Little, show manager of the Chicago Gift Show, with a note that said, "It isn't too often two nice people come down the pike with a unique gift product." (It was unique, alright, dried mushrooms.) "You cannot always tell from the first show. You may want to reconsider and try it one more time." Our logic: here was a man who saw thousands and thousands of gift items in his travels and in the shows that his company managed across the county. I said, "If he thinks our products are unique, then maybe we should try it one more time." That note from Mr. Little gave us new encouragement, and off we went to Chicago the second time.

Keep in mind, his nice note was not necessary for him to keep the show full since there was a waiting list of people who would have been happy to take our place.

As before, we got help from the ever-willing and eager doorman to get our items in the big exhibit hall. This time, along with product and exhibit cartons, we had a lovely antique pot with a flower in it to dress up our display area. But going through that fancy lobby in the Palmer House, that pot fell off the cart, broke into many pieces, and left a pile of dirt on the floor and a limp, wounded flower. What a mess. How embarrassing. These country girls weren't making a very good impression in the lobby. Here's the rub about dragging all that stuff through the lobby. After we were in the hotel (our second show), we found out about a loading dock in the back of the hotel, where we could've easily unloaded our product. Ah yes, a best-kept secret with the doorman. Guess what, the doorman saw an extra dollar sign when he helped with all the luggage. Yep, the country girls got hoodwinked. The unloading dock was free.

Alright, now we were in. We were nervous and a bit anxious about how business would be this second time.

On with the show! We set up a beautiful display, arrived early the first day of the show, waited with anticipation for the show to begin and for the arrival of the first buyers. And arrive they did! The show opened with a bang. We had buyers waiting for us to write their orders. We tripled our business from the first show. What was the difference? Who knows? But the fact is that a word of encouragement to try one more show put us and our business onto a whole new track. Thank you, Mr. Little!

As Overly-Raker grew, we exhibited in many Little Brothers trade shows.

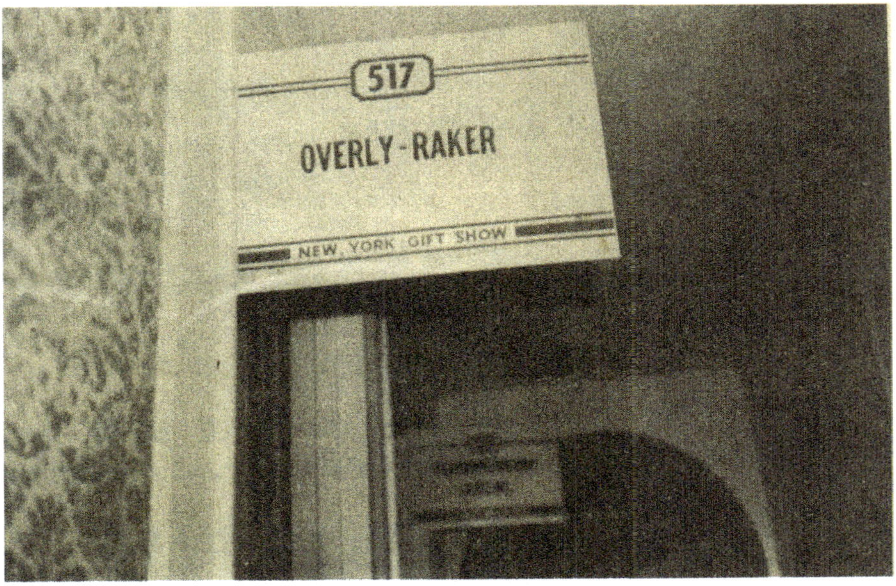

Printed with permission from Fulton County News

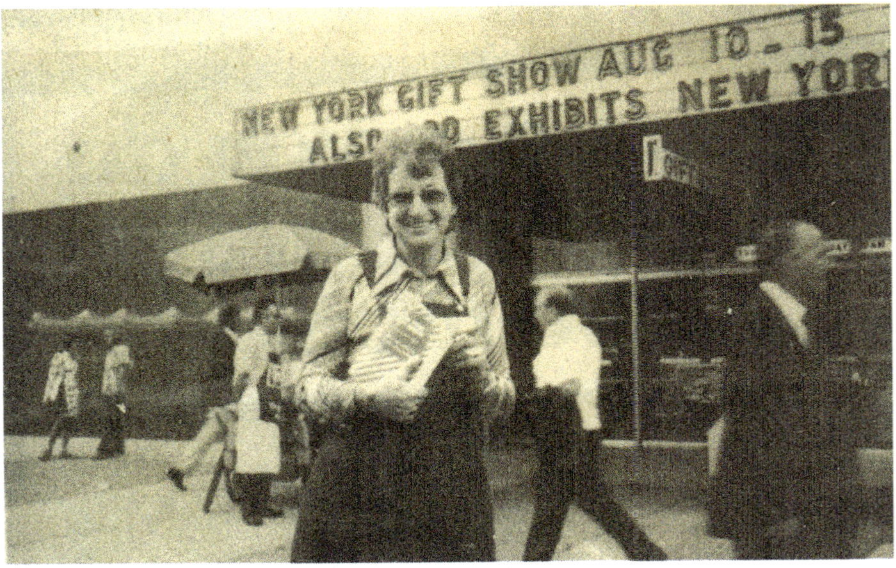

Helen heading into the gift show.
Printed with permission from Fulton County News.

CHAPTER 11

First Woman President of the Chicago Gift Show

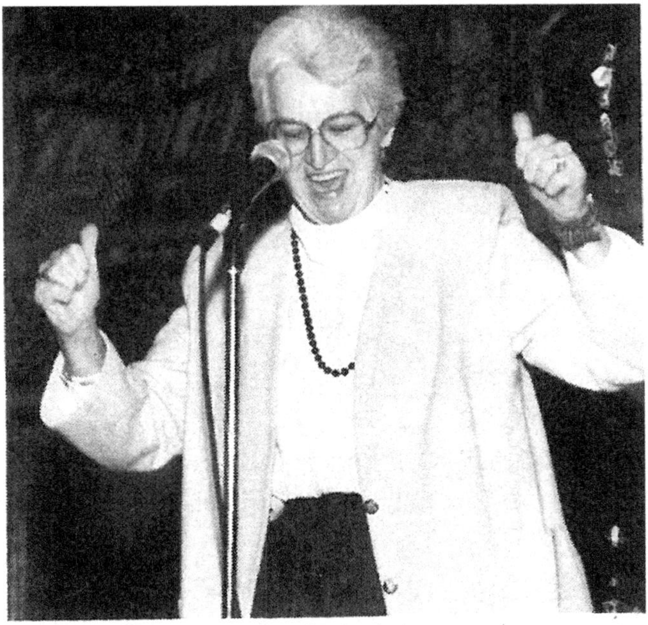

• Helen Overly, newly elected vice president, gives thumbs up to the "new" Chicago show.

Printed with permission from Fulton County News

The gift market in Chicago was always our best. We traveled to New York, Atlanta, San Francisco, Dallas, Philadelphia, and Atlantic City and had showrooms in Ohio, Minneapolis, along with sales reps throughout the country, but the market in Chicago was always our very best.

Unlike other major trade shows, that show was the oldest gift show in the country and was owned by the exhibitors. However, it was organized and managed by George Little Management Company, formally the Little Brothers Company.

There was a board of directors who were chosen from its exhibitor/members and met regularly to approve and suggest directions to the management team. Every six months, there was a member meeting. Freda and I had attended those meetings.

In the early eighties, Freda and I were exhibiting at the Winter Show in Atlantic City. We were still "small potatoes" and not real knowledgeable about the big world of trade shows even though we had attended the Chicago and Philadelphia Gift Shows. It was during that Atlantic City Gift Show that Mr. Bill Little, managing director of the Chicago Gift Show, came into our booth to speak to me. His words were "Congratulations, you have just been voted in to serve on the Board of the Chicago Gift Show." Goodness, I was so shocked I didn't know what to say. I honestly didn't know what a big deal it was. I wasn't sure how to act. I remember I was rather nonchalant about it when in fact should have shown more excitement. But who knew? I definitely felt out of my league. In the end, it was an honor indeed.

That day was the beginning of my journey on the road that led from board member to being elected to vice president and, ultimately, to the presidency of the Chicago Gift Show.

It was an honor to serve as the first woman president of the Chicago Gift Show. I was in good company, along with some of the heavyweights in the gift industry at the time. The president, when I served as VP, was Victor Matz of Kirk & Matz Ltd., a successful business. Others serving on the board during my tenure were Barbara Bradley of Vera Bradley fame, Russ Berrie, Allen Malmet of Esco Products, Sig Lang, Jay Monaghan, Douglas Stevens, and Ronald Jedinski.

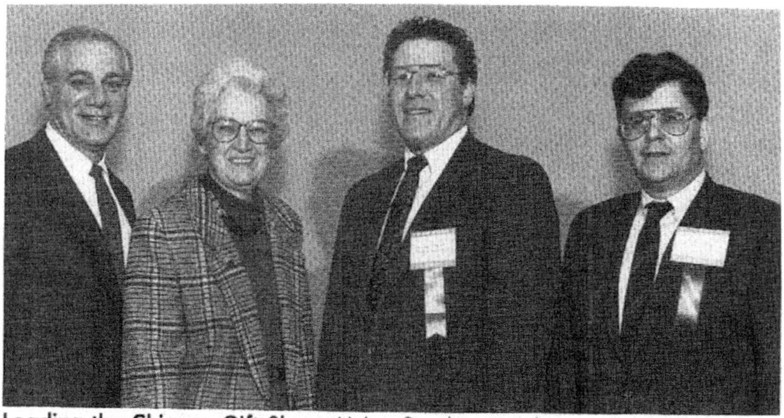

Leading the Chicago Gift Show. Helen Overly, recently named president of the Chicago Gift Show, flanked by the organization's new vice-president, Allen Malamet, left, the retiring president, Victor Matz, and managing director of the show, Will Little of Little Management. Overly, the first woman president of the CGS, will serve for three years.

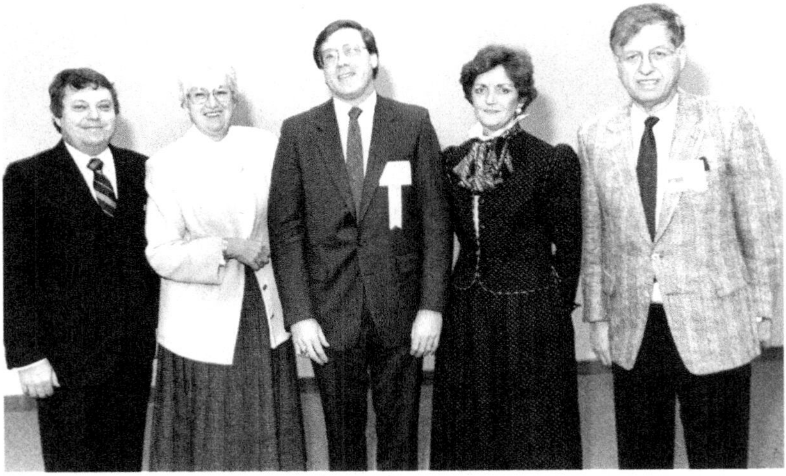

Ronald Jedinski, Helen Overly,
Victor Matz, Barbara Bradley, Russ Berrie

So for six years, three years as vice president and three years as president, I spent countless hours working to make the Chicago Gift Show the best in the industry. There were lots of meetings with show management, fellow exhibitors, and of course, the buyers. But here is the fun part.

This was not a paid position, but it had some neat perks. As the VP and the president, I received complimentary hotel rooms during the shows. Since our show brought in many buyers, the hotels treated us very well.

The first year as a VP, when I went to check into the Hyatt Hotel, I gave the desk clerk my name etc. She said "Just a minute" and disappeared into the office. Suddenly out came one of the management staff to "welcome" us to the hotel and escorted us to our room. A suite!

After she left, making sure everything was acceptable to us, Freda and I looked at each other and laughed like kids who just won free tickets to an amusement park.

That was just the beginning of special treatments for us. For six years (two times a year), we were given lovely hotel accommodations in different hotels. Our favorite was the suite we had in the Drake Hotel, one of Chicago's prestigious, elegant hotels. We were escorted to the room that happened to have the name, on the door, the Governor's Suite. Guess he was out of town. It had a large foyer, two walk-in closets, a huge room with a large oval table that would seat twelve, two seating areas in the living room to accommodate multiple visitors. Of course, a large bedroom with a beautiful bathroom. These experiences showed us how the famous live.

Since we were experiencing this and it didn't cost us anything, Freda and I decided we would spend some money and entertain the twelve sales reps who were in the city to help us at the show. We had room service at that big oval table. What fun to share with our friends!

When two of our young women reps arrived, they exclaimed, "This foyer is bigger than our whole room." That was the fanciest suite we had. Did I mention it had a doorbell?

Oh yes, at each of these different suites, on the day we moved in, we were the recipients of some sort of treat. It ran the gamut from a tray delivered with fruit and/or cheese and crackers to lovely trays with fresh flowers, a bottle of wine, gourmet chocolates accompanied with lovely, fresh fruit.

Pretty snazzy, huh? The bottom line: we were given wonderful experiences that we could not have paid for! Blessings abound!

As written in the *Chicago Gift Show Bulletin* on March 7, 1990:

> When questioned about how it feels to be the first woman President of the Chicago Gift Show, she immediately smiles and says she is not a newcomer to firsts and prefers to think of herself as a businessperson and another in the long tradition of member-exhibitor Show Presidents. "After all," she states with good-humored irony, "I was recently honored with the first Man of the Year Award of my business community's Fulton County Chamber of Commerce in Pennsylvania."
>
> Helen Overly is President of Overly-Raker, Inc., manufacturing more than 300 different products from decorative home accessories, stuffed toys and holiday decorations to baby items. The firm markets its line nationally and is a long-standing member of the Chicago Gift Show.

One thing that being the first woman President of the Chicago Gift Show proves is that this Show is open to new opportunities. It certainly says that this Show recognizes the importance of women in our industry and in its future. In a way, it goes back to using the environment of the Show as a business mode: The Chicago Gift Show is in sync with its times.

When asked what she hopes can be her contribution to the Chicago Gift Show, she answers, "I want the Chicago Gift Show to be THE place that Midwestern buyers and business owners come to buy products, understand new trends, learn about the industry, enjoy themselves, and be the basis of making more sales and profits for each of their stores."

New Chicago Gift Show President Makes Positive Changes

Helen Overly is the new president of the Chicago Gift Show. As vice president of the Show for the past three years, she comes with a wealth of experience and a decidedly enthusiastic—as well as realistically optimistic—point of view as to what her leadership period can accomplish.

"The Chicago Gift Show has many unique virtues that are now totally in sync with the times. But, perhaps most important of all is its tone; its approach to product, visual merchandising and service is uniquely its own and can very much be a merchandising model for our times," states Overly.

She continues to explain that, at a time when all retailers are having to rethink their marketing approaches to address a new decade and era of selling, the "friendliness of the Chicago Gift Show experience" among fellow member-exhibitors and exhibitors and buyers can be adapted to buyers' own retailing environments to create more sales and profits. "It is my hope that positive attitudes and service can be examined in seminars. This would be another way the Chicago Gift Show goes further to support its attending buyers' businesses."

Also in sync with the times are the mix of classically best-selling gift products, with the ever-important new product introductions, continues Overly. "The show offers companies that are old friends with best-selling lines and new introductions. Equally important are the new companies which the Chicago Gift Show constantly searches out—keeping the exhibition vital. All buyers have to do is visit 'The Best of the New' to find some of the outstanding new companies who are exhibiting at the Show. We're the only gift show in the country with that feature!"

When questioned about how it feels to be the first woman president of the Chicago Gift Show, she immediately smiles and says she is not a newcomer to firsts and prefers to think of herself as a businessperson and another in the long tradition of member-exhibitor show presidents. "After all," she states with good-humored irony, "I was recently honored with the first 'Man of the Year Award' by my business community's Fulton County Chamber of Commerce in Pennsylvania."

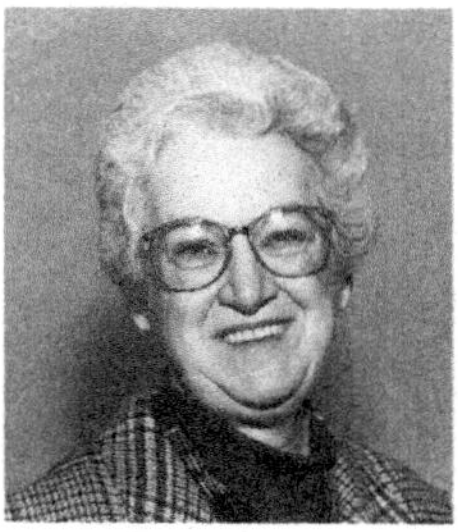

Helen Overly

Helen Overly is President of Overly-Raker, Inc., based in McConnellsburg, Pennsylvania. Manufacturing more than 300 different products from decorative home accessories, stuffed toys and holiday decorations to baby items, the firm markets its line nationally and is a long-standing member of the Chicago Gift Show.

Giftware News, June 1990

Printed with permission from Giftware News

Fulton Co. News 3/6/91

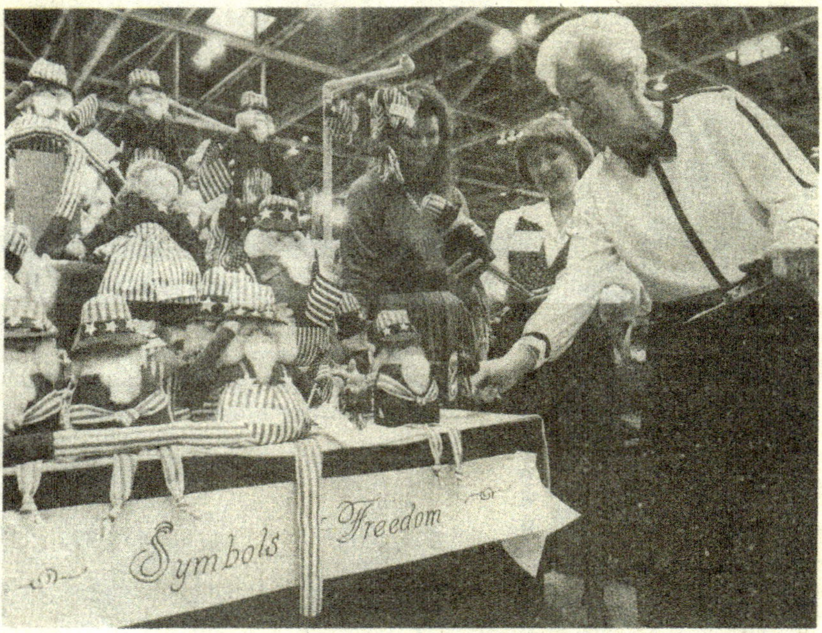

Helen Overly, president of Overly-Raker, Inc. of McConnellsburg shows the O-R line of patriotic items at the Chicago Gift Show which was held at McCormick Place in Chicago during the week of Januay 27, 1991. The local soft sculpture manufacturer now offers the "Symbols of Freedom" line pictured above and although the line was designed and introduced prior to the Gulf War, Overly reports that sales of the timely items have been "brisk" and that Overly-Raker like all other American patriots are having difficulty in procuring American flags for their line. The line includes: Top, left to right: Uncle Sam Chill Chaser and Uncle Sam collectible dolls; Middle Row: Miss Freedom and Roly Poly Uncle Sam; Bottom Row: Floppy Uncle Sams and "Salutin' Sam." The line also features a cat named Sam and a smaller cat named Sammy. The above photo appeared in the Tuesday, January 29, 1991 edition of the Chicago Tribune.

Printed with permission from Fulton County News

CHAPTER 12

Be Creative Even When You Have Goldfish in Your Gutters

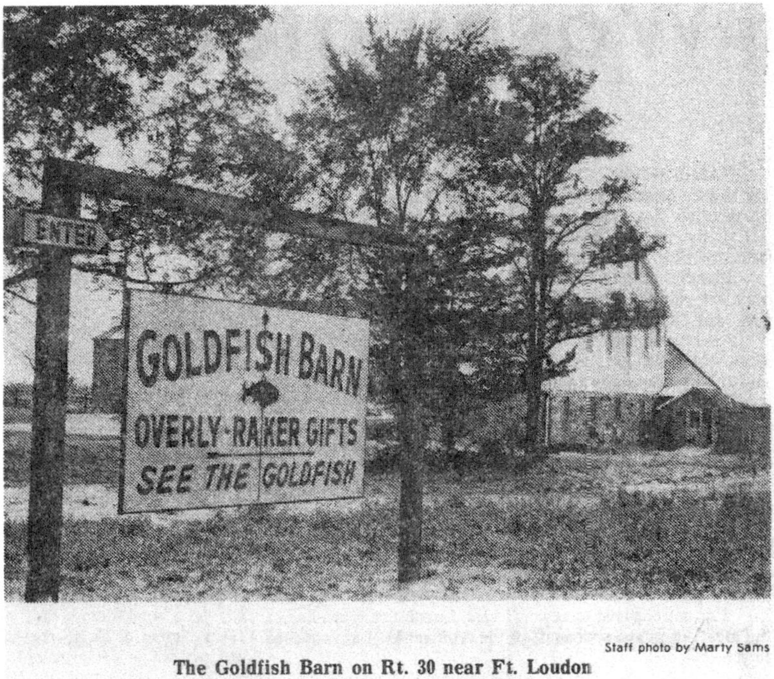

The Goldfish Barn on Rt. 30 near Ft. Loudon

In 1976, the owner of a nearby goldfish hatchery, Richard Rice and his wife, Sue, were frequent customers to our showroom/village. Our wholesale business was still in its infancy, and our retail showroom kept us fed. Remember, I like to eat.

They had just bought a farm with a lovely old barn. They decided it would make a neat gift shop. It was a great location, on highway US 30 (opposed to our rural current location). They asked us to consider opening a gift shop in the barn.

Freda and I went to see the barn, which was surely a barn, smell and all. You have to know I was never around animals and a barn, so it looked pretty dismal to me. However, Freda, the visionary, saw potential, discussed it with me, and I actually thought it would be a good idea also.

Now where to start? First idea. We have never determined who had the idea, Freda or Dick, to clean the manure gutters and have goldfish swimming in them. One of them, positively.

Having goldfish in the gutters came about because the Rices owned a goldfish hatchery, where they raised millions of goldfish a year. Their goldfish were shipped all over the world, an interesting story in itself, but I must move on to the barn cleanup!

Now some of you may not know what a manure gutter is. I didn't. It is an area designed into the floor of a barn to clean out the sewage left daily from the cows. Cleaning the gutters was left to Dick. He had them cleaned, scrubbed, and painted a lovely light blue.

Our job was to clean the walls and ceiling and construct displays etc. Cleaning a barn was a new experience for us. Did you know that cows can actually get "that stuff" on the ceiling? That was a mystery to me until it was explained. The cows are lined up with back end toward the gutter and, at unpredictable times, could swish their tail around and, yes, you guessed it, splatter that stuff on the ceiling and walls. Now that was an education for us. But how to get it off?

While others were celebrating Fourth of July 1976, Freda, sister Dorie, and I were decked out with old clothes, rubber gloves, large mops and brushes, and Top Job. Scrub we did, most of the day. Rubber gloves were good, but we had water running down our arms way past the gloves. What a job! I wanted to do a commercial for Top Job. It worked, with a lot of muscle and determination with it! Oh, but the barn smelled good and began to look like we could begin with the construction of display fixtures. We also had the floor cleaned and carpeted.

Now the fun began. We looked for old tables, cupboards, and chairs for display. We also had some displays made by an entrepreneur, Ed Guion, from the Lancaster area in Pennsylvania.

A challenge. The gutters lined the shop perimeter and were filled with water and beautiful fish swimming in them. Now how to get across them (about eighteen inches wide) and also how to keep people from falling into them. Creative thinking. We built little bridges across traffic areas and hung planters and fixtures in low-traveled areas to keep customers from mindlessly walking into them. The barn was ready now for displaying our carefully selected items. We were doing all this along with the Overly-Raker Village and wholesale business. Busy people we were.

The entrance to the gift shop was through the old milk house. The old milk tank had been replaced by a hand-thrown stoneware fountain in a pool alive with beautiful koi. The main shop had the wooden bridges for crossing, and there were goldfish swimming throughout the gift area. We sold hanging aquariums, baskets, toys, sterling jewelry, pots, leather, and a little bit of everything else we found interesting and unique, especially unique.

As we had planned and hoped for, Overly-Raker at the Goldfish Barn became a destination and was very successful. We were blessed with good employees to work with us. It surely took us some time managing to cover all the business that was happening. Overly-Raker Village, Goldfish Barn, and a rapidly growing wholesale business.

The barn was the place that set in motion soft sculpture. Freda thought we should have some animals like a cow, a horse, a pig, and yes, a frog and a fish. All these she would develop patterns for and make one of each. My job was to find fabric for her. Patchwork was very popular then. I called a fabric distribution center in Harrisburg to find patchwork fabric. I found we would need to buy a whole bolt of cloth, which was twenty-five yards. I was thinking, how would we ever use twenty-five yards of fabric? There were two patterns of patchwork available, and the salesperson asked which one I wanted. Hope you understand, I was on the phone. What would you do? I bet, like me, you would say "Send me the most popular."

As long as we had a few animals, we decided to take a couple of samples to the Chicago Gift Show along with a very big display of Realies. We had a small display of soft sculpture animals. To define soft sculpture, I always tell people to imagine a bronze or wooden sculpture of a horse. Well, we did the same thing but only with fabric and stuffing.

TRIBUNE-REVIEW — MONDAY, APRIL 16, 1979

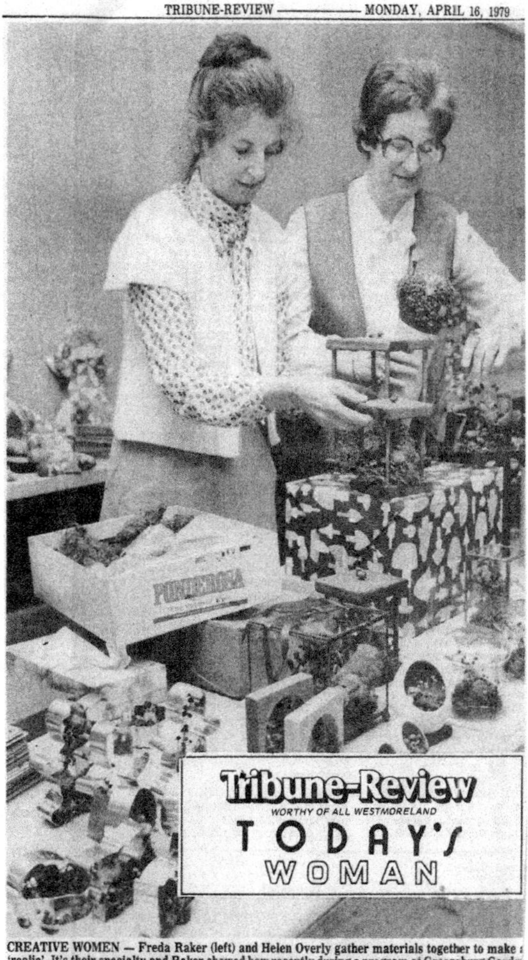

CREATIVE WOMEN — Freda Raker (left) and Helen Overly gather materials together to make a 'realie'. It's their specialty and Raker showed how recently during a program at Greensburg Garden Center which was part of the garden center's semi-annual meeting. All sorts of examples of 'realies' are shown in the foreground. 'Realies' are made with dried mushrooms. (Photos by Warren Leeder).

Printed with permission
from Tribune-Review

We took, maybe, six pieces and a large display of Realies. Interesting to us was that the animals had appeal to every buyer. So with that success, Freda designed another two or three pieces, and then it was the task of getting them sewn and stuffed.

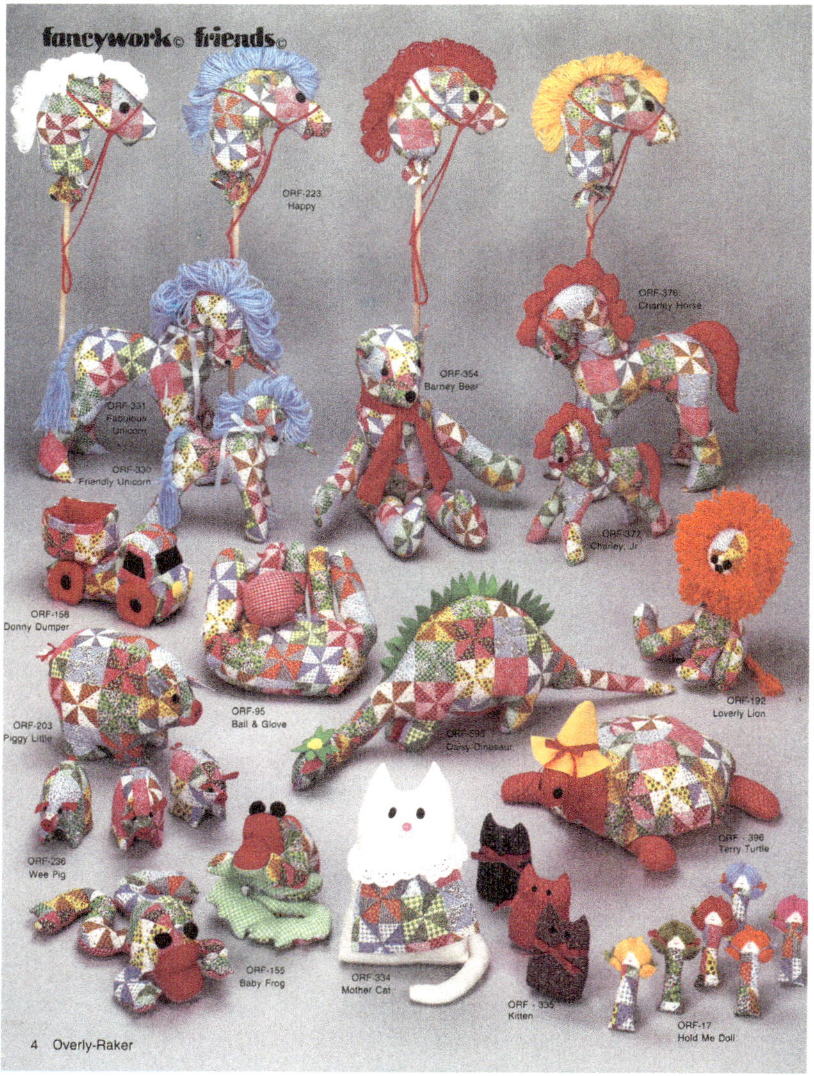

Early patchwork friends

CHAPTER 13

Patchwork Fabric, Birth of Soft Sculpture, and More Growth

There is an additional story to that twenty-five yards of patchwork fabric that I thought we would never use. Actually, that material became almost a trademark of Overly-Raker for some years. We made a whole line of animals, from kitties, pillow dolls, turtles, frogs, to rocking horses and added a baby line with baby quilts and pillows. Yes, patchwork was hot.

Designer's idea. Why not make a line to decorate the kitchen. Why not? Kitchen appliance covers for every kind of small appliance along with patchwork placemats and napkins. These items were in demand especially since the mail order catalog, *Miles Kimball*, picked them up for their catalog.

Oops, another mountain loomed in front of us. *No more patchwork* in the marketplace. What to do? Leon, that ever-present purchasing agent, spent time on the phone and finally found a company that would print the fabric for us. Oh great! But one small, little hurdle. Did I say little? Yes, we could have it printed, but the minimum order was twelve thousand yards.

Here they are, in-house orders, lots of them, but not twelve thousand yards worth of orders. What to do? Cancel the orders or take it on the chin and order the fabric. That meant $12,000 for fabric all at one clip, money we really didn't have.

My philosophy was, always, if we needed raw material for anything to make the product, we should buy it. So yes, we ordered the fabric. Orders came in fast and furious. We often commented to each other that every house in America must have patchwork appliance covers and/or placements.

Wait, I am not finished with the patchwork fabric story yet. Before it was all over, we had two more printings done, a total of thirty-six thousand yards. Remember when I said I was not sure we could use twenty-five yards? Moral of this account is, don't be afraid to step out in faith into the unknown. What if we had decided not to print the fabric and cancel all the purchase orders we had waiting to be shipped? You answer the question!

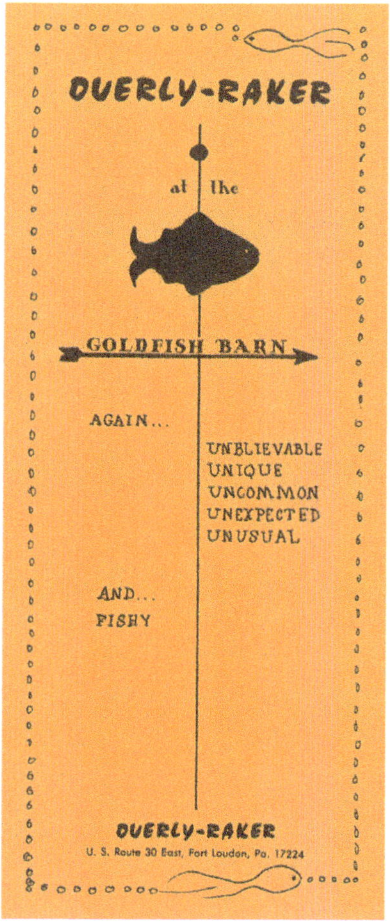

Original brochure

Fabric items would be the launching pad for our company to add another dimension, soft sculpture. Eventually, we would leave the Realies. We became hugely successful both locally and around the world for our soft sculpture.

I always maintained that the Realies took a discriminating buyer. But after a couple of years of Realies, we introduced the soft sculpture to the gift show and the retail market.

Thus, a whole new product line was born. Sad to say, in 1979, when we had to move to larger quarters, the Realies had to go. Mainly because they were dirty and fabric items had to be in a clean environment.

In 1979, we began creating *only* soft-sculpture items, and we were able to move out of our basement to an actual office/manufacturing space with over 3,300 square feet. We were so excited with all this space. However, our excitement lasted only for a little over a year. By 1981, we had completed a 6,000-square-foot addition to this first little building we bought.

Business flourished until we outgrew that manufacturing space too, and in 1983, we rehabbed the original building and added another 7,200 square feet. What started out as 3,300 square feet ultimately grew with three additions to be 26,500 square feet. A happy home for manufacturing Overly-Raker soft sculpture.

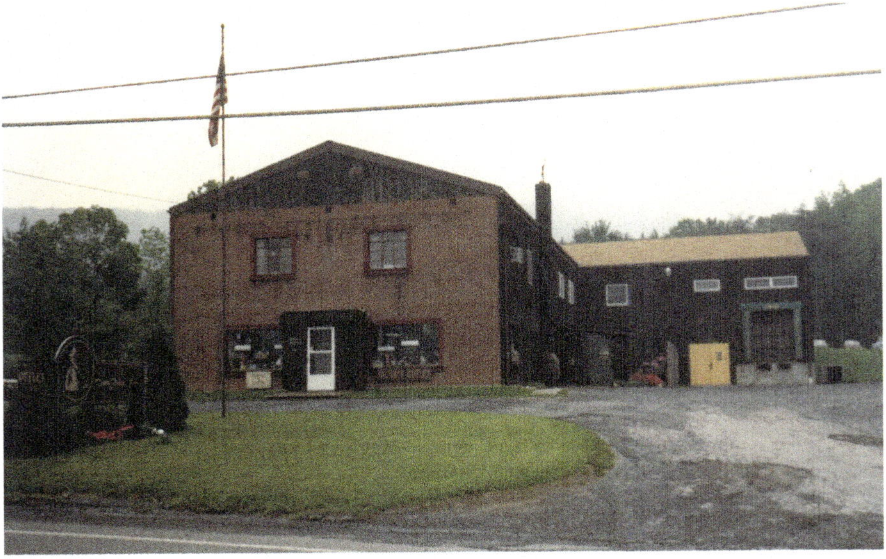

Overly-Raker building

How to Cut Large Volumes of Fabric: Another Challenge

But with every step of growth, there seemed to be a different challenge. I told you about the thousands of yards of fabric. What I didn't mention was how to cut all that fabric. While we were still working (manufacturing) in the basement, remember we also had the retail business. God seems to have answers to our challenges in the most unlikely places or persons.

A saleslady, Joan Steel, went to our retail shop to sell us handmade pillows and beautiful handmade skirts she had made. As always, we were interested in what she was doing versus the kind of things we were making, and a conversation ensued about how to cut layers of fabric. We had fast graduated from the hand scissors. Now don't you know she had the answer?

Joan described this nifty little electric knife she found that could cut up to twelve layers of fabric at a time. Wow! Twelve layers at a time? She described it to look sort of like a pizza cutter. The wheel, extremely sharp, would spin very fast and whizz right through the fabric. I bet she was not out of our driveway until I was on the phone, trying to order one. Actually, we learned it was called a sample cutter, which large factories used to make small cuts.

Before it was all over, we had bought three of these sample cutters. Actually, Janet Souders, one of our workers, took a fabric cutter and a sample cutter home and cut fabric pieces on her kitchen counter/island. That was in the midseventies.

Thank you, Joan, for introducing us to that fantastic little machine. Joan and we became longtime friends. I even helped sell her business, A Pretty Penny, in about year 2000, give or take a year or two.

If you are laying out fabric in layers, you need a large table to cut it. We had heard about a sewing company going out of business. Certainly, we should go and look to see if they had anything we could purchase.

Just smile here. Such a bargain for eighty feet of cutting table. We bought it! That is the good news; the bad news was we had no place to put it. The space we had would accommodate only thirty feet at that time.

Finally, after our expansion, we had plenty of space for the cutting table. But one more thing. That little sample cutter was just that for us, a sample cutter. Our need far exceeded what it could do.

We put our purchasing agent, Leon, on the job to seek out large cutters. His research ended. We purchased two very large cutters, also called knives, that allowed us to layer up one hundred layers of fabric and cut through them. Since we ordered production in dozens, we usually layered ninety-six layers.

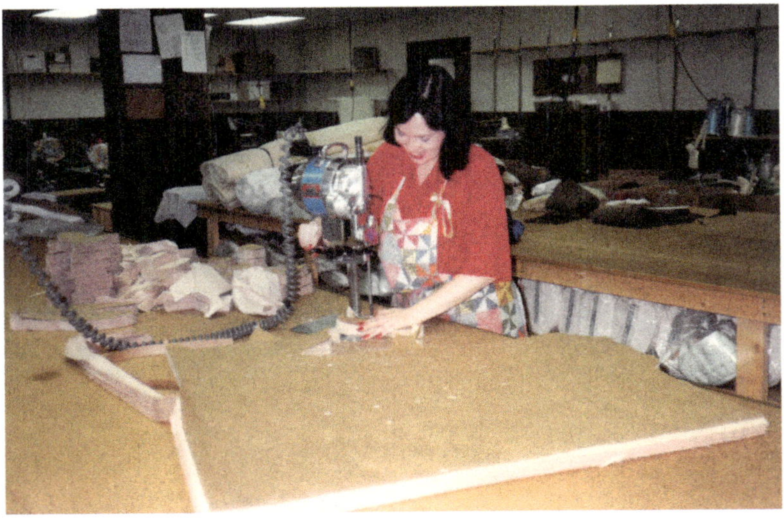

The cutting knife in action

Now this new cutter/knife necessitated we install three-phase electricity into that area of the building and also needed some training for our cutters.

Love this, we had a man from an NY garment factory come to train our two young women cutters to use this machine. All went well until they showed him some of the very small pieces we needed to cut. His reply was "It can't be done with this cutter." Never tell these women it couldn't be done. They figured out a way to do it. Thousands and thousands of small pieces were cut over the years. They did what the expert said could not be done.

CHAPTER 14

More Learning for These Two Entrepreneurs

Even after we participated in our first two or three gift shows, there was a lot of learning for these two manufacturing ladies in the wholesale gift market. We assumed that the gift shops would order their Christmas inventory at the July/August markets. In those days, we were selling mostly to small mom-and-pop stores. But no, we found after the first couple January markets that buyers wanted to see our new Christmas line in the winter market (January/February). That meant jumping ahead a year with new designs. For us that meant probably twenty to twenty-five totally new Christmas designs to show along with our current collection.

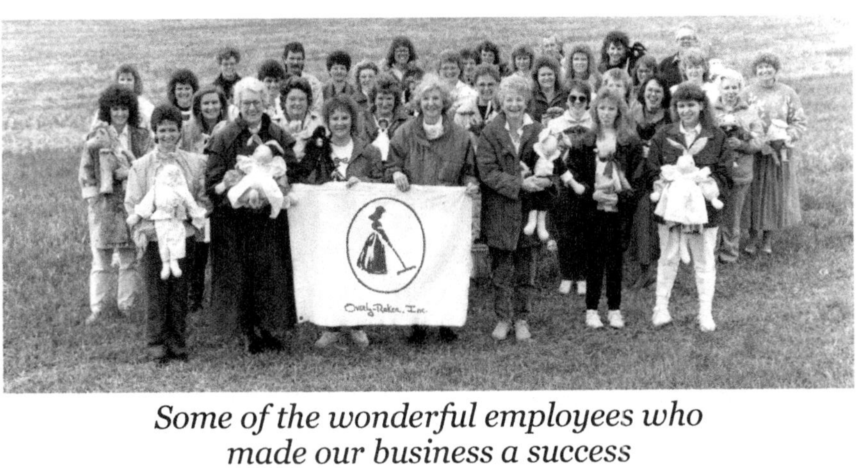

Some of the wonderful employees who made our business a success

Freda was our lone designer at that time. Over the years, we had help in the design department. However, everything pretty much went through Freda's head and eyes; thus, our line continued to have a unique look, a personality of its own. Only one designer had the "Overly-Raker" look. Freda's niece, Kate Gamble, came to work for us in the design department, and I actually could not distinguish her work from Freda's. That special creative gene ran strong in the family.

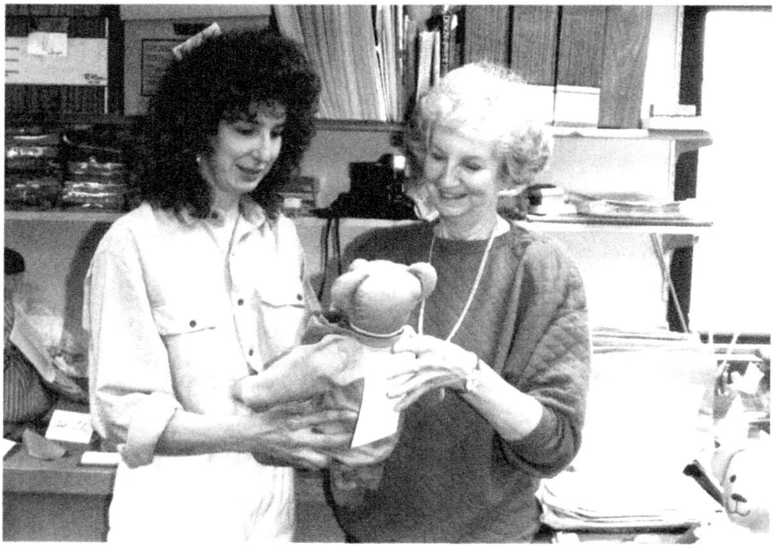

Creative minds: Freda with Kate Gamble

Mattered not if it was our Christmas and collectible Santas and angels line or the massive Halloween line or the everyday line—all were distinctively Overly-Raker. These traits I called the Overly-Raker personality. We stayed true to our brand. That is what the market liked and bought and what grew our business.

Over the years, Overly-Raker designed, developed, and brought to the market place nearly four thousand items.

In the beginning, we named our soft-sculptured line Overly-Raker Friends. And didn't we make friends all over the country! As our business grew, the tag line on all our catalogs was "Still making friends."

As written by Bill Callen, *Public Opinion*, on November 25, 1987:

Overly-Raker "Makes Friends" in Holiday Market

It's odd, really, but Helen Overly looks almost like someone would imagine a modern Mrs. Santa Claus, from the snow-white hair and red-rimmed glasses to the easy, welcoming smile.

Overly and her partner Freda Raker, who doesn't look like Mrs. Claus, form Overly-Raker Inc., a soft sculpturing firm whose slogan is "We Make Friends." Indeed, they've made lots of them.

Soft sculptures, those items most of us know as stuffed animals or dolls, are extremely popular holiday items.

Last year, Overly Raker made nearly 300 soft sculpture nursery-rhyme decorations for holiday display in the White House. The company's handiwork is not headed for Washington D.C. this year, but the United Parcel Service trucks that visit the plant three times daily indicate that business is fine without the federal government patronage.

"It starts in July," Overly said about holiday orders and shipping. "In August it builds, September is very busy and in October it's just wild."

Among the company's clients are J. C. Penney, Montgomery Ward and the Museum of Natural

History in New York City, which bought a shipment of soft-sculpture dinosaurs.

The company's 40 full-time employees work in brightly colored, warm surroundings, stitching, stuffing and packing items that will be distributed nationwide to retail and specialty outlets in time for the Christmas crunch.

In addition to crafting soft-sculpture figures, the company silk screens and makes Christmas stockings and ornaments. While many corporate heads busy themselves forecasting the stock market and fretting over its decline, Overly and Raker must, as early as the previous January, guess whether geese, sheep or another item will be in demand next Christmas.

"Geese have been popular the last four years, but we think they're beginning to diminish slightly," Overly said. "Dinosaurs are big now, even for Christmas, and we think sheep will be coming in big next year."

Figures show they have not been guessing wrong too often. Between 1978—the year before Overly and Raker took their business from the basement of a house and into a former dairy distribution center—and 1986, sales increased 1,600%.

Overly said 1987 sales, almost all of which are wholesale and 65% of which are holiday goods, likely will top $1.7 million, a one year increase of some $23,000.

The physical plant has undergone two major renovations since Overly-Raker bought it in 1979. What was a 3,300-square-foot facility is now

17,300 square feet. And still not big enough to accommodate the company.

"We're again out of space and wondering what we are going to do," Overly said. "We never seem to have enough space."

Overly and Raker, whose corporate symbol is a woman holding a rake inside an oval (get it?) started their business in McConnellsburg 14 years ago.

Raker left her job as an executive secretary at DuPont in New Jersey and Overly bade farewell to teaching to start the venture, which, in its first year, grossed about $15,000.

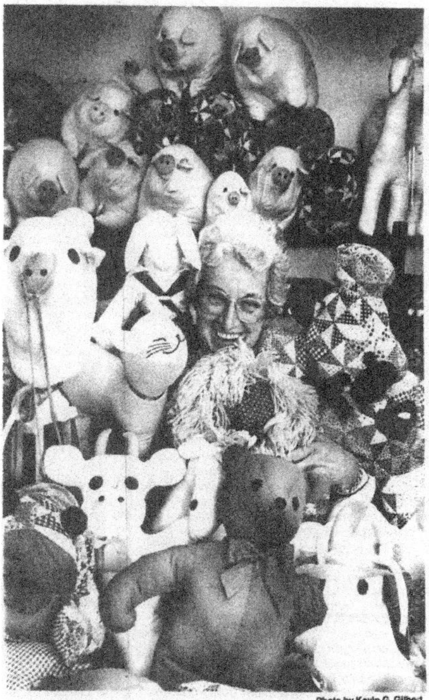

Photo by Kevin G. Gilbert

Helen Overly is lost among her soft-sculpture dolls

Million-dollar industry

Printed with permission from Fulton County News

CHAPTER 15

Fast-Forward: Bigger Space, First Private Label Order

> Persistence was important in their success. Their fledging, two-person craft business stumbled into a 36,000 piece order for Christmas sachet ornaments from Carolina Soap and Candle, a national distributor.
>
> —Abby Schultz, *Berkley Springs Journal*

Smelly Pellets

Back to Chicago for the third time, and we had a new exhibit area. We now needed two booths, which were 200 square feet of booth space instead of just one 10' × 10'. Sure enough, with the request for additional space, we were moved up with "big guys" in McCormick Place exhibition hall.

This move was a learning experience in many ways. One, we were surrounded with larger manufacturers and some importers who taught us the ways of bigger business. And two, we had enlarged our product line with some pillow dolls, some short and chubby, some tall and thin, and then just a little, tiny doll that we called a "hold-me doll," just right for a little child to hold on to and even keep in their pocket. Now that we had larger exhibit space, we took a large branch from the woods behind our house, painted it white, and used it for displaying the little hold-me dolls. We hung them rather like Christmas tree ornaments.

This display caught the eye of a buyer from a large company at that time, Carolina Soap and Candles. This company made all kinds of fragrance items, and this buyer had the idea that we could put fragrance in this little hold-me doll and use it as a Christmas tree ornament. The buyer approached me and asked, "Have you ever considered making a product for another company?" I hadn't considered it before, but I quickly considered and said "Oh yes." His next question was what the price would be if he bought in large quantities. Honestly, I had no clue. I told him I would have to go back to the office and look at costs and give him a quote. He never said how many he might want, and I never asked. Can you see what big-time operators we were not?

We were all excited about this idea but went on with the show, which turned out to be a very good one. Sales were going up rapidly, which meant lots of work when we got home. By now, of course, we did have some inventory to ship out, but the demand was increasing with sales from this market.

When we arrived home, the first thing, along with increasing our production, was to look at our costs for the little doll and send a quote to this buyer. Faxing off the quote (no Internet or e-mail in those days), we eagerly awaited his reply. The reply was not what we wanted to hear. The quote for hold-me doll Christmas ornaments was too high, but he suggested perhaps we could make another item (less money) that could be filled with a sachet fragrance to use as a tree decoration and later be used to hang in a closet or place in a lingerie drawer.

Off went that request to the designer, Freda. She came up with a new item, Christmas bow tie sachet, and sent it to the buyer again but this time at much-less cost. As usual, when you're doing a design for a company, you went back and forth with fabrics and design until they were approved, and then the big shocker. Remember, we were still working in a basement when we got a call from the Carolina company purchasing agent. That was big-time for us, a call from a person's job titled *purchasing agent*. He told me that we would be getting a hard copy, but for starters, he wanted to get this in production now, and they would like thirty-six thousand pieces. My answer? "No problem!" Oh my, I had no idea what a problem that would be.

Remember I told you we were with the big businesspeople in this new exhibitor space and particularly next door to an importer. I overheard them talking about their "lead time." Bear in mind I was from academia (not business) but assumed that that meant how long they had to get the product from offshore to their warehouse. Not wanting to appear like a small-time deal, I said to this purchasing agent, "What's my lead time?" Suddenly a shock went through my body. Maybe that wasn't the correct terminology. Well, fortunately for me, it was correct, and he told me when they expected delivery of the order.

Add to this order, the deal was we would make the item and Carolina Soap and Candles would supply the fragrance to be inserted into each piece. No problem! Well, no problem until, one day, I heard what sounded to be a big truck.

Now picture this: we live in the woods, up a long driveway that was cut through the woods, with not a great deal of space for large and high vehicles.

Now there might have been a problem. I saw this eighteen-wheeler come up our driveway, literally filling up the space between the trees. I said, "What in the world is that thing coming up here for, and how will he ever get turned around?" Well, up he came. He jumped out of the truck and said, "I don't know what you have here, honey, but it sure does smell good." What we had here was, get this, one ton of sachet. Yes, I said *one ton.* Now I ask you, where would you put a ton of anything in your house? And our house was already filled up with "business" stuff. The saving grace was that the sachet was packaged in three-foot-square cartons. We unloaded them and moved them in every space available—some into Freda's mother's garage; some in our basement and anywhere possible.

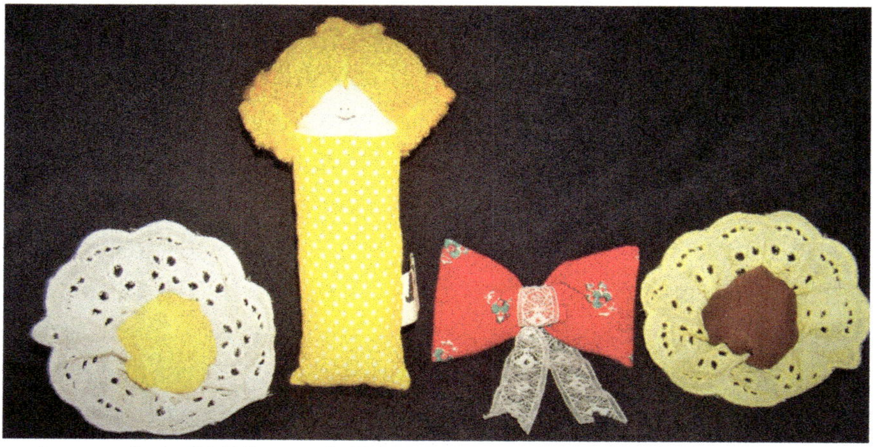

Daisy sachet, hold-me doll, bow tie sachet, yellow daisy sachet

Let me describe these little sachet tablets. They were about the size of little saccharin tablets (if you can remember them), and they were *extremely* fragrant. I termed them smelly pellets. That's forever the term used in my mind or anyone else who helped us with them.

Well, now that we had the smelly pellets, we could begin production. I use that term *production* loosely. Freda had this great idea that we would make them all ourselves and that would give us a real financial boost. No need for extra payroll. Remember, she was the artist, not the businessperson, but I sure went along with her idea. Sounded great to me.

She had to do twelve samples for photography. First problem. We had to get Christmas fabric when only spring was available in New York at the fabric market. She and I spent three days in NY finding samples and making decisions for this order.

She had already developed the learning curve with the samples she made for photography. For the first twelve samples, she took the fabric, which she had cut into rectangle pieces, folded it, sewed it, turned it so it made like a little tube where we could put in the sachet and then fold each end into the center. Now tie that with a piece of lovely white lace. Looks like a little bow tie. Beautiful but lots of steps, lots of labor. Next twelve samples, how to streamline for production. This time, the fabric would be stitched on the right side then no need to turn since the raw edges would be folded in anyway. Great! Now the third twelve. Aha, she didn't even need to sew them. Fold the fabric to make the tube and glue it. Insert the sachets, fold in the ends, glue, tie the lace bow, and presto, we had it.

Now back to this production we could do ourselves. Great idea! Since it was spring and the fragrance was too overpowering in the basement, we set up shop on the deck outside. Four of us, Freda, her mom, sister Dorie, and me. Off we went!

After the first two hours, I was already bored with it and was the self-appointed runner to answer the phone, count and package, or make coffee when necessary.

By the end of the first week, we had 500 pieces made. Only 35,500 to go. *Help! Five hundred made and 35,500 to go!* To give you an idea of what 36,000 pieces required: it is over one thousand yards of fabric, eight hundred yards of lace ribbon, and nearly one ton of sachet pellets. Obviously, we needed to increase our production in order to meet the time frame that we had agreed upon.

I remembered we had had two ladies, Janet Souders and her sister-in-law, JoAnn Souders, come to us and asked if there was anything they might be able to do at home. No, we had nothing like that. But suddenly those ladies came to my memory. Perhaps they were still interested and this would be the perfect item for someone to do at home.

That was the beginning of our "homeworkers." Who knew what a big impact this decision would have on not only our business but the whole community?

We called the ladies, explained the process of making these little items, gave them the price, and yes, they were interested. We had precut the fabric. I often say it was pretorn fabric. We didn't have any big fabric cutters in those days and found, if we made the first small cut properly, the fabric would tear into the width we needed in long lengths, and then we would cut it into the dimensions that were needed for the sachet. So we armed these ladies with the "precut" fabric, a large spool of the lace, some glue, and yes, a box of smelly pellets. I often said, if we had opened all those boxes of the fragrant pellets at one time, we would've smelled them all over Fulton County. It turned out that these ladies had an aunt and a sister-in-law who would also like to make these items for us, and so off they went with more cut fabric, a roll/spool of pretty lace, glue, and a box of smelly pellets. With the help of about fifteen ladies working in their homes along with us, we were able to meet the deadline required for the first shipment of sachets to Carolina Soap and Candles.

But wait, the story of sachets and smelly pellets is not over.

After the Christmas bow tie sachets, Carolina Soap and Candles asked us to come up with a spring item to make into a fragrant sachet. Freda designed a couple of things, and one was a little daisy made with white eyelet with a yellow center.

They loved it and, from that, developed a whole line called Fresh as a Daisy. The first sample we sent was a lovely little sachet with white eyelet with the yellow center, and that was fine. But they got back to us and asked if we could also do the daisy with a yellow eyelet with brown center. Sure, no problem.

Oops, there was a problem. We looked everywhere we knew to find yellow eyelet the same size and pattern as the white. There seemed to be none available. (There was no Internet then to search for these items. We were limited to only the distributors we knew or could find.) So the next best thing, we certainly would not say we couldn't do it. Here we go again, making the impossible possible. We bought white eyelet, thousands of yards, and dyed it yellow. That became my job, dyeing white eyelet into a pretty yellow.

So the first step was to roll off several yards, put them in the washing machine, very hot water with yellow dye. It came out just beautiful, perfect color. Now it needed to be dried. I put it into the dryer, which I quickly learned was a big mistake. When I opened the dryer, I had one big ball of yellow eyelet. I could find no end to even begin unraveling it. Problem solved. I had to just cut it somewhere to start unraveling it. Oh no, not an easy task. Rethink this thing. Good news. The eyelet needed to be cut in twelve-inch pieces. So I began to cut them, but because it was all in a big ball, the eyelet needed to be ironed. Have you ever tried to iron eyelet that was all gathered? The iron seems always to want to go into one of those holes of the eyelet. Talk about a learning curve. New procedure the next time. I precut the eyelet into the twelve-inch pieces we needed then tied them in a bundle of ten, put them in the washer, and when I got them out, I just hung them over a drying rack, where they hung, dried perfectly, and did not need to be ironed. That was a huge time saver. I might add that, this time, Carolina Soap and Candles only wanted 25,000, not 36,000. We made 12,500 of each color of daisy total 25,000.

Mission accomplished!

CHAPTER 16

It's Fun Working with the Big Dogs

Somewhere along the way, I think in NY, the buyer from Fabergé saw us and asked us to make samples of angels to be packaged with their "touch of class" cologne for the Christmas season. After we made several angel samples and priced them, they gave us the order: 144,000 pieces (our largest order ever).

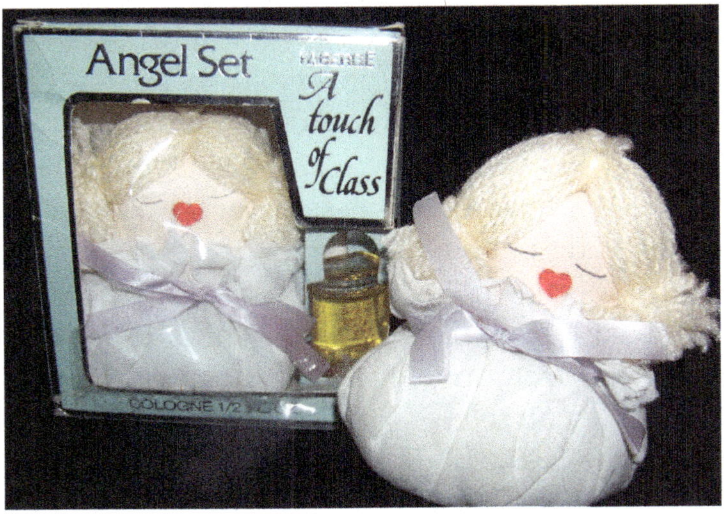

Fabergé angel

Wow! As we started production, we sent production samples to the buyer, Louise Caputo. No, they were not quite right. The neck was too skinny. She was right. Ever see a choking angel? We corrected them, and then the neck was too thick, but with several tries, we finally had production just right.

After several weeks of production came the next problem, where to store the angels until the shipping date. Ah yes, Freda's office, since she spent most of her time in the design studio. We could stack them in her office. Remember, we were in full production with our regular product line too. As I went checking to see how the production of the angels was progressing, I saw Freda's office was nearly full. I was so excited thinking we were making great progress. We had hired a project manager, Joyce Mellott, just for this special production. I spoke with Joyce, "This is great. How many have we made?" The reply, "Ten thousand." I was amazed, surprised, and in shock. Only 10,000 and the room was full? Oh no, we still had 134,000 to go. Where in the world were we going to store these until we got them all made? Next challenge.

The owner of the local grocery store, the IGA, had just built a new building and moved his market into it. The old building was still empty. Perfect, maybe. I called Ray Koontz, a very seasoned, successful local business owner. I was a new, fledgling business owner and was rather timid calling him to ask for space. When I mustered up enough courage to call, I explained our dilemma of lack of space and our need for temporary storage. He was a man of few words. Yes, we could have some space. The bigger question for me was the cost. When I asked him the cost of renting, he replied, "How much do you want to give me?" I had no idea what the market rate was and what he would expect, so finally, I said, "Would a hundred dollars a month be enough?" He immediately said "That will be OK." I knew then as I know now that that was a gift to us. The space was worth far more, but he wanted to help us. He became a wonderful friend.

Back to the angel production. They had special packaging, first in a retail box to include the bottle of perfume and an angel, then those boxes had to be placed in a master carton. Every couple of days, we would load up completed cartons in our van and take them about two miles into town for storage at the former IGA facility. To finally give you some idea of what 144,000 angels, boxed and ready for shipping, might look like: it took two tractor trailers to haul them away.

An additional funny story. When the first tractor trailer came to pick up the angels, it had Fabergé advertising painted all over it, Burt Reynolds and Farrah Fawcett pictures and all. I was impressed that here it was, backing up to our dock, so I took a picture. The driver of the tractor-trailer truck looked at me, said, "Didn't you ever see a tractor trailer before?" I laughed and replied, "Not with Fabergé at my door."

That was the largest private label job we ever did. It was done and delivered on the date we promised. We always took great pride that we never made a commitment that we did not keep, even if it meant working late at night or lots of overtime.

As if the order of angels were not enough, along with our regular product line, we also had a special order from Procter and Gamble. So simultaneously with the angel order, we also made a colorful big lion and a frog. Procter and Gamble was doing a toy-box promotion and was filling it with different toys. They gave us an order for 500 of each, lion and frog. Fortunately, we had rented that storage space for angels, and we also needed it for these large items as production was being completed. That was an amazing year for Overly-Raker.

Tupperware and Private Label

We had the good fortune to do several private or specialty products for companies. You have already read about the sachet (smelly pellets) for Carolina Soap and Candle, the angels for Fabergé, and the lions and frogs for Procter and Gamble. We even made a specially item for the Girl Scouts of America.

Along came Tupperware. They asked me, "Could you make a chicken or hen out of your patchwork material?" Absolutely, no problem. Their company was promoting hen parties and wanted five hundred chickens.

Now to Freda, the design department, to make a sample chicken. Then to price it and get back to the buyer. That was my job.

I was excited about the design and the reasonable price we had for them and called the purchasing office in Florida. I gave the lady the price, which she was happy with. Then she said, "Could you fly it down to me"? Somehow that touched my funny bone, and I said, "If I can get it started in the right direction." Think about it; we were here in a rural area with no airports close by, so flying it down to her struck me funny. However, I would check and get back to her. Remember, no Internet or smartphone to send a quick picture.

I knew of a small airport in Hagerstown, Maryland, about forty miles from us, who handled air freight. We packaged the chicken ready for shipping. Dorie was assigned the job of taking it to the airport. Never having done this before, she finally found the place and then had papers to fill out. A gentleman was helping her, and he asked, "What do you have in the package?" and she answered, "A chicken." That set off a round of laughter in the office. Finally, all was done, and off went the chicken to Florida.

Did they like the chicken? We sent a cute, slick chick, and that was *not* what they had in mind. They wanted a plumper chicken. Oh, now back to design. We actually made three designs, and each time, they needed something changed. Finally, I got frustrated and told them we were sending a final sample and would not be able to do any more changes.

Amazingly, when they were aware of our frustration, they decided on a hen. *But* no, we were not finished yet. Could we make little peeps to go with the chickens in different fabrics? And oh yes, "Could you find a way to attach the peeps but also allow them to be removable from the hen?" Never say no to a challenge. We did it. That clever designer, Freda, made darling little peeps and attached them, one on each side of the hen, with Velcro. It worked; they were happy with five hundred hens and one thousand peeps. Another mission accomplished!

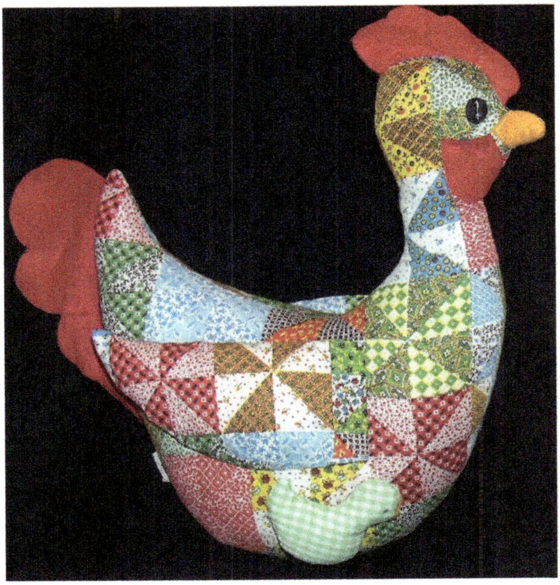

Slick chick

Doing private label can be challenging but has its rewards too. We have met many nice people along the way.

While we were producing our own product line, we were approached at one of the trade shows by the World Doll Company, which had the trade rights to produce Clark Gable and Scarlett O'Hara dolls along with Elvis Presley. Could we make the costumes to fit the dolls? We made samples and got the job.

You can guess Elvis was the big seller. The likeness of these dolls to the real characters was extraordinarily good. These were high-end collectible dolls, and every detail in the costumes was done with great care. Only our best sewers could make this delicate work.

We made four different costumes for the Elvis doll. If you are an Elvis fan, you may remember what he wore. There was the white leather-like costume with some red trim and a scarf, a black with silver trim, and the iconic gold suit. The gold fabric was really expensive. We made one thousand each of the black and white but only five hundred of the gold.

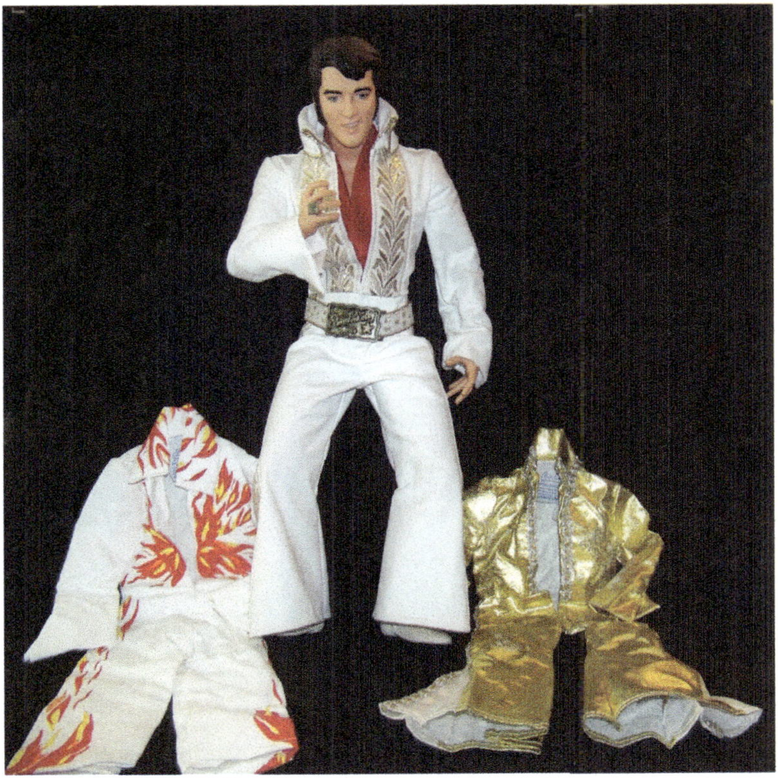

Elvis and his many outfits

That was a fun project!

CHAPTER 17

The White House

Overly-Raker is the largest maker of soft sculpture gifts and decorations under one roof in the country. One year they even helped to decorate the White House for Christmas.

—Arthur Ciervo, *Pennsylvania Magazine*

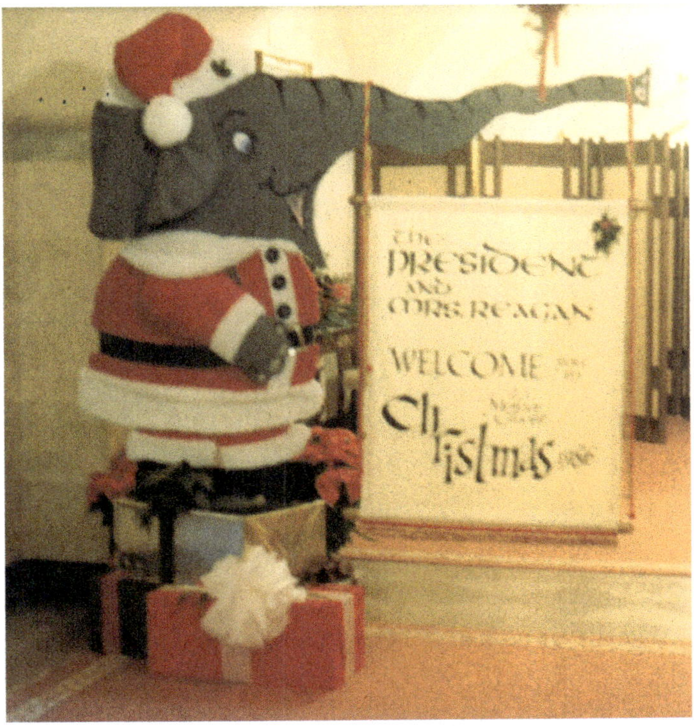

Ladies and gentlemen, right this way.

You never know where your next step in business will lead you. In our case, it led us to the White House.

Freda and I were at the Washington Gift Show in January 1984, exhibiting our spring and summer products. A woman came into our booth, looked around, and then asked to see our Christmas catalog. I told her that we had not yet printed it and asked for her business card so that we could send it to her when it was released. She said, "I don't have a business card. I'm from the White House," and then she added, "*The* White House."

I didn't know what to say and then came back with "Oh yes, I've heard of that place." I thought it was funny. I laughed. She didn't. I assumed that would be the end of any contact with that woman. I had given her our spring catalog, so she had our name and address.

In March, a call came into our office from someone who wanted to speak to the president. That would be me. My secretary buzzed, saying that Nancy from the White House was on the phone. This was when the Reagans were in the White House. This call was not from Nancy Reagan. It was from Nancy Clark, who wanted to speak to me. When I got on the phone, she said, "I spoke with one of your representatives at the Washington Gift Show." That would be me also. But I didn't tell her I was the one and the same, for fear she would remember my flip comment.

We chatted for a bit, and then she asked me to give her a price for an item that would be three feet tall and not sure how big altogether. This was a somewhat vague request. I told her I would not be able to do that unless we actually made the piece to figure out how much fabric, stuffing, etc., it would be. I told her that we were just north of Hagerstown, Maryland, and said, "Why don't you come up and see us?" Surprisingly, she accepted with enthusiasm, consulted her calendar, and told me which times they were available, and we decided on a date. She called back later and said Mrs. Reagan's interior decorator also wanted to go, along with the "head usher" of the White House. The more, the merrier.

We were all pretty excited at Overly-Raker, knowing we were going to have guests from the White House. Since we did not have many choices of restaurants in our area, we decided to have lunch for our guests at our plant. We had lots of good cooks and employees who were more than happy to participate in making the lunch, serving the lunch, etc., for visitors from the White House.

Upon their arrival, we gave our guests a tour of our facility, showed them what we did, how we made our items, etc., and then began to discuss what they wanted us to do for them.

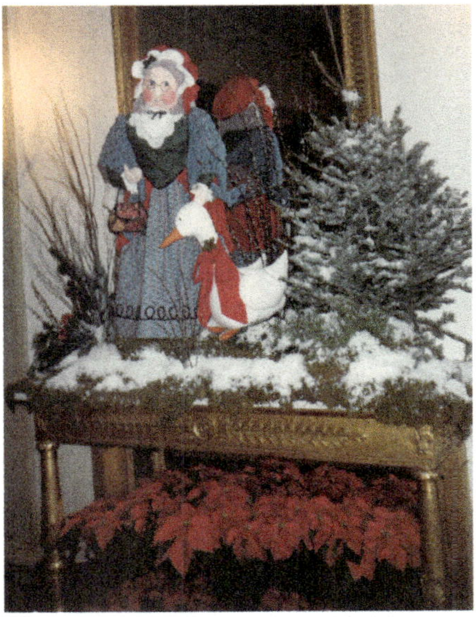

Mother Goose keeps you on the path.

Mrs. Reagan wanted "a Christmas morning in the nursery" as her theme for the White House decorations. Nancy Clark had seen a cute Humpty Dumpty we already had in our product line. That was what spurred her interest since she was thinking of nursery rhymes. And Humpty Dumpty happened to be one of them. Mrs. Reagan's decorator wanted us to make the characters using illustrations from an author who had just done a book on nursery rhymes with wonderful illustrations. Freda reminded him that those would be copyrighted and we would not be able to copy them.

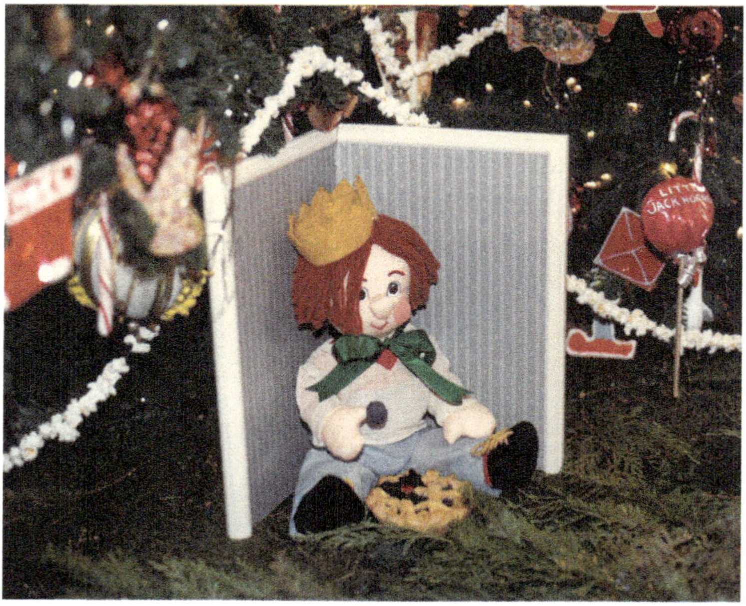

Little Jack Horner and his Christmas pie

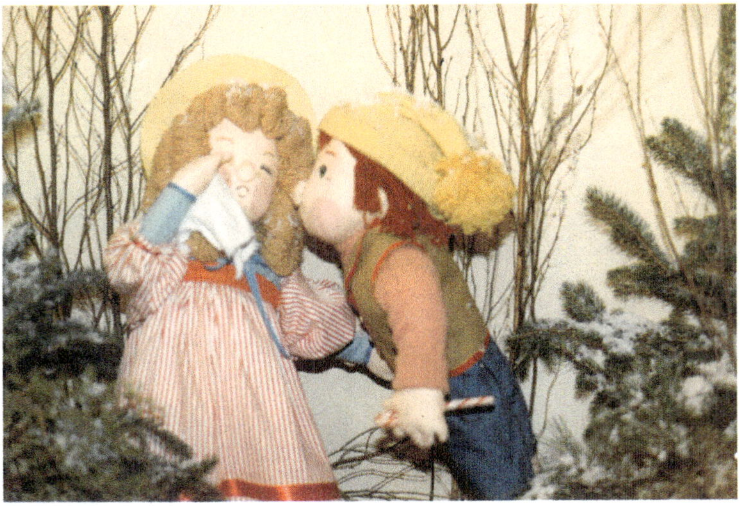

Georgie Porgie at it again

The decorator said, "Oh, this author will give us permission I'm sure because it's for the White House."

But guess what? That author was not impressed and refused permission to copy them. That was neat because then it allowed Freda to do her own designs. Freda and the design staff, then Kris Earley, Joyce Mellott, and Janet Souders, made every conceivable nursery rhyme character (three hundred pieces in total) you could think of: Three Blind Mice, Humpty Dumpty, Cow Jumped Over the Moon, Jack Sprat Who Ate No Fat, on and on. We made a large five-foot Mother Goose for the entrance to greet people who came to see the decorations. We followed that up with little geese tree trims for the Christmas tree in the Blue Room.

The Christmas Tour of the White House opened to the public on December 7, 1986. On December 20, *Christmas in Washington* aired on network television. During the special, First Lady Nancy Reagan hosted a tour of the White House, which featured all the decorations.

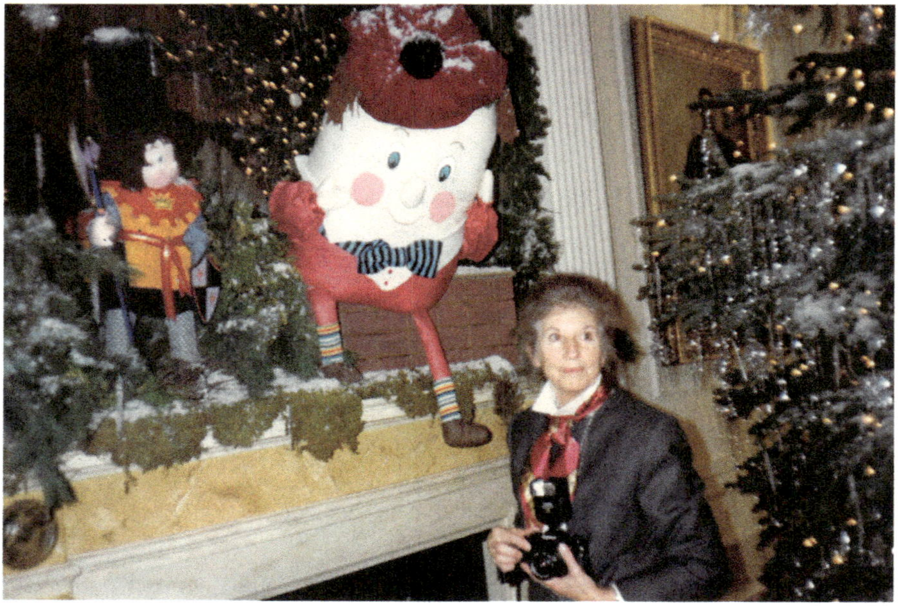

Humpty Dumpty watching Freda

A Funny Side Story

After these preliminary plans were made, Freda and I traveled to the White House with a sample Humpty Dumpty. This Humpty Dumpty had to be large to sit on the mantle in the East Room. The problem was the East Room mantle was only eighteen inches deep. The Humpty needed to be a big character yet still able to sit on the mantle. We brought this big sample along with a couple of other things to measure and see if they would fit. White House security knew we were coming; they had our driver's license numbers, our social security numbers, and we thought it would be easy to get in through the gate. Not so. We stood there with our bundles of things, and the guards wanted to see our driver's license numbers (did I say it was raining?) and we were trying to juggle these bulky big objects together with our handbags to get at our licenses.

We finally dealt with that and got into the guardhouse. Then the guards needed to pass a wand for security over Humpty. Turns out Humpty was too fat and they needed to call in a K-9 dog to sniff him. Fortunately, they let Freda and me go in along with the other samples. After we had been taken to where our items would be placed (we needed to get an idea of size), we went down to the flower shop in the White House, and there sat Humpty. He had finally gotten clearance.

Overly-Raker was the featured Christmas decor at the White House in 1986. After all the production labor and shipping, the installation went off without a hitch. As a surprise to our entire staff, we chartered two coach buses to take them to the White House for a private tour. The decorators were there to meet us and answer all our questions. What a thrill for all of us.

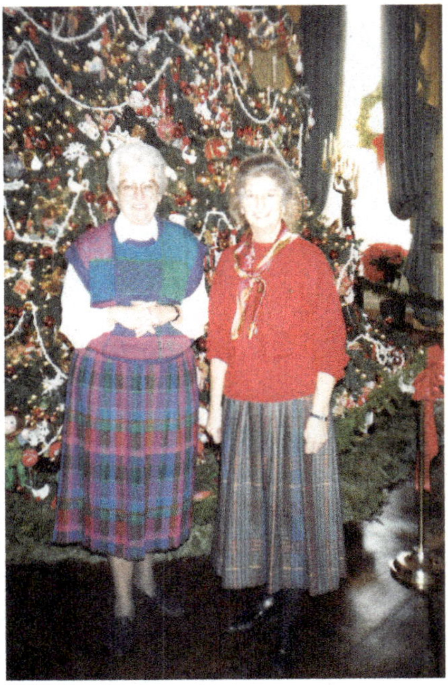

Overly-Raker tours the White House.

Surprises Abound from Both Employer and Employees

It was not always us going above and beyond to show our employees how much they mean to us.

One example. They typically made wonderful Christmas gifts for Freda and me.

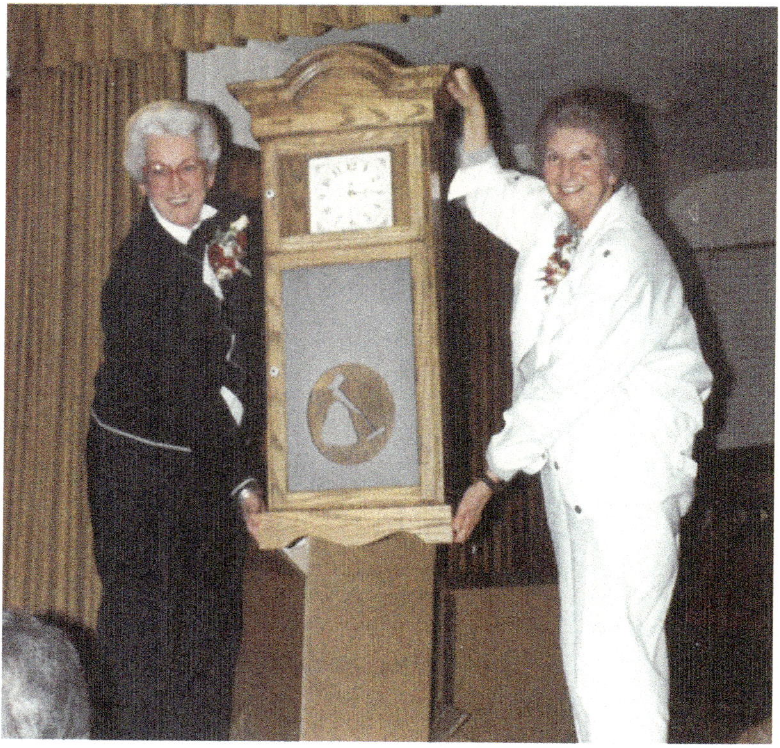

Thanks, employees! We love it!

Also, to celebrate our fifteenth year in business, our employees surprised us with a limo ride to a banquet to celebrate this business milestone.

O-R Marks 15th Year With Banquet

By Jean Snyder

Over 80 employees, friends and family members of Helen Overly and Freda Raker attended a surprise banquet and party in their honor at the American Legion Home on Saturday evening, April 16. The event was organized by O-R employees to celebrate the fifteenth anniversary of the Overly-Raker business. The business, located just north of McConnellsburg, is now one of the largest soft sculpture businesses in the country. It was started in April of 1973 by Helen Overly and Freda Raker in the basement of their home and has continued to grow by leaps and bounds to its present status. Overly-Raker provided the decorations for the White House Christmas of 1986.

The banquet and party were attended by present and past O-R employees and featured a meal followed by entertainment presented by O-R employees.

Helen and Freda arrived by "stretch limo" complete with red carpet. They were escorted by Kate Gamble, her husband, "Babe" and Gary Cunningham, limo owner and driver. Cunningham, a former Fulton Countian and former employee of O-R, owns the limo business in the Lancaster area. The impressive white limousine is an exact replica of the personal limo owned by New York/Atlantic City business tycoon, Donald Trump.

Following the meal, O-R employees Janet Souders, Dorie Fell and Kate Gamble were featured in a parade of successful Overly-Raker items. Janet Souders modeled the famous patchwork designs which were popular items in the early Overly-Raker line. Dorie Fell modeled the Faberge angel and Kate Gamble appeared as the legendary "Elvis doll." Leon Hurst served as master of ceremonies for the evening.

With Sandy Miller at the piano, Linda Mapstone and Leslie Souders presented "a look back," a hilarious and touching medley of songs describing the "good times and bad times" during the Overly-Raker years of business.

Linda Mapstone also presided over a game of Overly-Raker bingo using bingo cards to display the many items in the Overly-Raker line that have been successful and also "not so successful" during the past fifteen years.

Original Overly-Raker employees were honored at the head table and they included Jean Kies, Betty Cunningham, Kathleen Sprowl, Dorie Fell and Marge Chamberlain.

O-R employee, Joyce Mellott, on behalf of all Overly-Raker employees presented Helen and Freda with a gift, a beautiful wall clock with pendulum, made in Wells Tannery, expressedly for Overly-Raker. The clock features the O-R logo on the glass door.

Both Overly and Raker, genuinely surprised by the evening, spoke fondly of their fifteen years and cited their employees loyalty and dedication as the hallmark of their success. Overly said, "without our employees, there would be an Overly and a Raker but there would be no Overly-Raker." They both expressed hope that there would be "fifteen more years, hopefully as good and rewarding as the past fifteen."

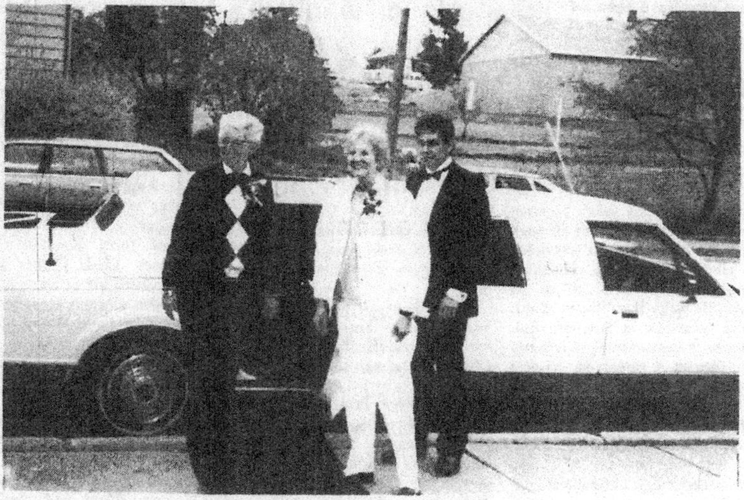

Helen Overly (left) and Freda Raker are shown here as they arrive by "stretch limo" at the American Legion Home on Saturday, April 16. Overly-Raker employees surprised their "bosses" with a banquet and party in celebration of Overly-Raker's fifteen years in business. Gary Cunningham, formerly of Fulton County, escorted Overly and Raker to the event in his "stretch limo." Cunningham operates a limo business in Lancaster, PA.

Printed with permission from Fulton County News

CHAPTER 18

New Product Every Season—Something Has to Go!

Success can, and most often does, create challenges. Certainly, that was our experience. Starting a small retail shop was fairly easy, but branching out to multiple retail shops (three) and a wholesale business was a different story. Developing, marketing, and advertising were a bit of a task, but here was the whopper. Developing a whole new product line for the growing wholesale market was a big one!

Keeping all the balls in the air with a growing little wholesale business is an unending hurdle.

New Designs for Soft Sculpture

Our need to be original and different in the marketplace with *new* was a huge task. Freda was the "head bean" in that department. She not only had to come up with the idea but also had to make the patterns, select the material, and make the final sample. I had ideas, but trust me, I could not have made it if my life depended on it! A multitalented, creative person filled the bill with Freda, the success of our business.

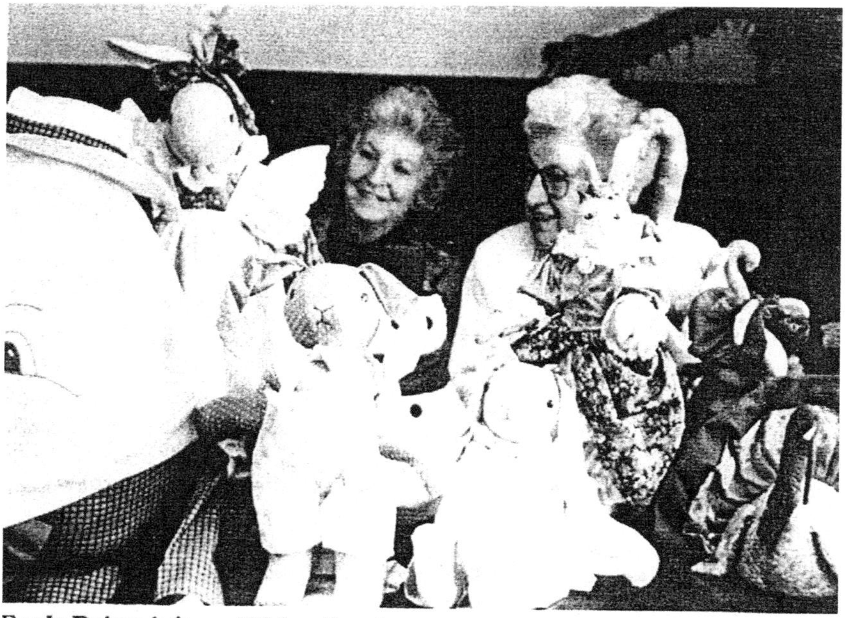

Freda Raker, left, and Helen Overly operate a McConnellsburg factory where the employees assemble soft sculpture. The firm is the largest maker of soft sculpture located under one roof in the country.

Printed with permission from Fulton County News

With retail business, it is possible to get the new product from many sources to meet the need or satisfy that customer who comes in looking for "what is new" in your store. But in manufacturing/wholesale business, you have to develop a new product all the time for each new marketing season.

As business grew in both areas (retail/wholesale), it became apparent something had to go. That was when Freda and I decided that retail had to go and all our efforts would be to grow the wholesale market.

Here is how the demise of the retail went. The shop at Raystown Lake was first to go. That necessitated moving that shop's inventory into the Overly-Raker Village and the Goldfish Barn. One down, two to go. Done!

Another year went by. Things got rather hectic on the home front at Overly-Raker Village where, along with retail, we were "manufacturing." We had run out of space and manpower. Decision number 2: close the village. We advertised and had a moving sale. We moved what was left after that sale to the one remaining retail shop, the Goldfish Barn. Two done, one to go.

Personally, I loved retail. I enjoyed talking with the people, helping them select something for a special person or occasion, but that fun had to be transferred to our blossoming, fast-growing wholesale business.

Number three, the final retail gift shop business was not closed. The best part of this was that one of the ladies who worked for us at the Goldfish Barn (who did a fantastic job), after some negotiation, decided to buy the business. Pat and Herb Bowling became the new owners in the early eighties. The business changed hands a few times but remained an ongoing business until July 2015, when the then owners, Dick and Sue Rice, after twenty years, decided to retire.

"A Barn, a Gift Shop, a Dream Fulfilled!"

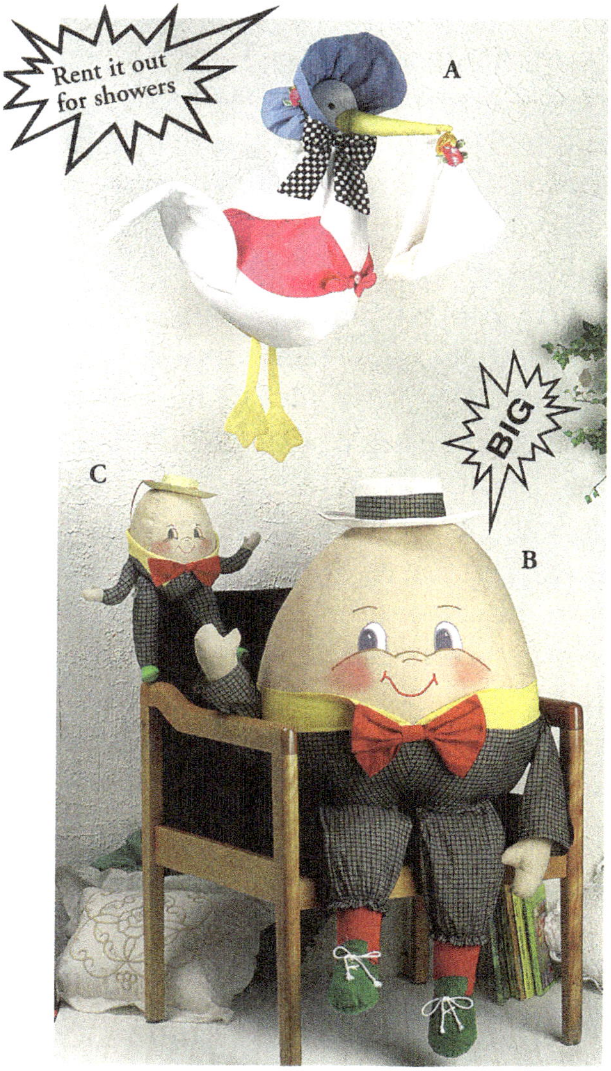

Overly-Raker's display figures offer great versatility for year-round use. The base figure is crafted from beige broadcloth and all clothing and accessories are removable. Five different costumes are available and made to fit the same base figure. This Mother Goose Display could be a witch for Halloween, a bunny for Easter or a Santa for Christmas. Your sales representative can show you all of the available costumes.

D) 3019 Mother Goose with Gander Mobile
27-1/2" H x 35" W

E) 3020 Mother Goose Display, 50" H
3021 Mother Goose Costume only

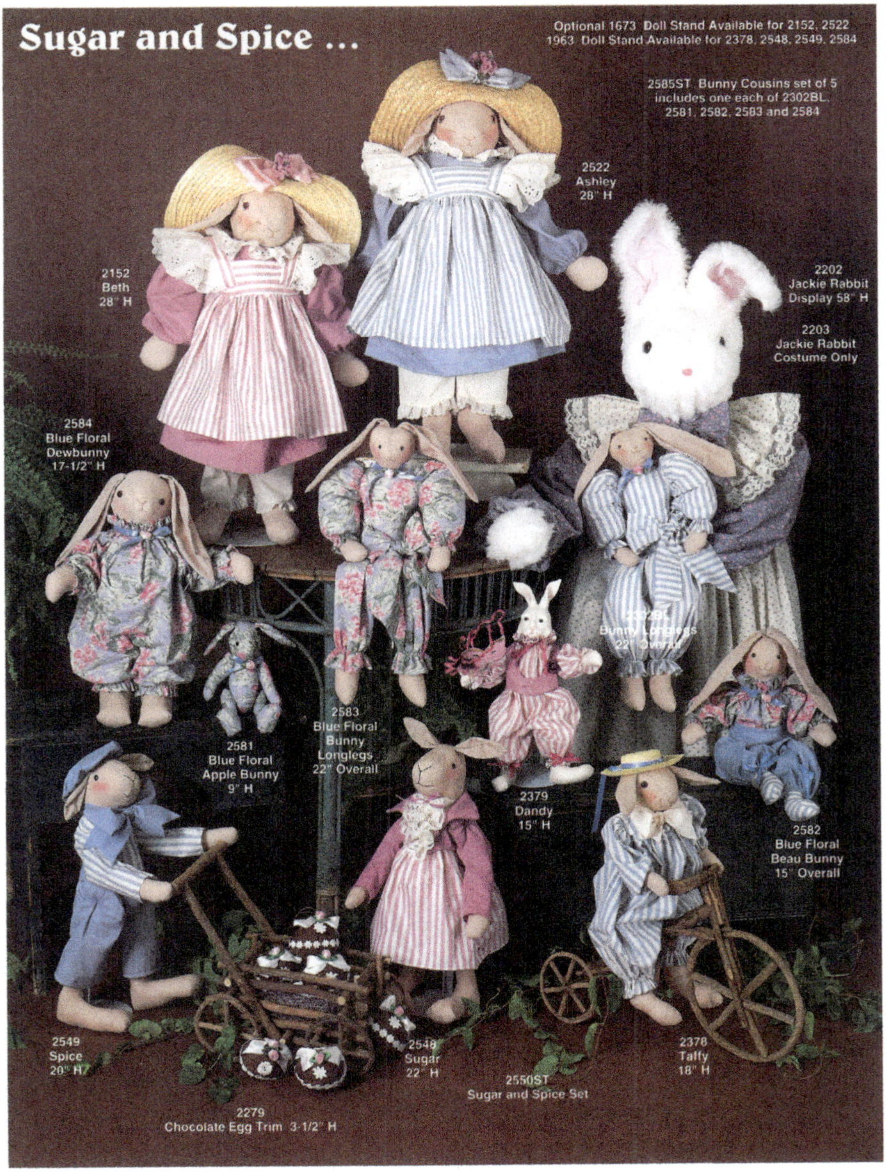

A peak at an Overly-Raker catalog page

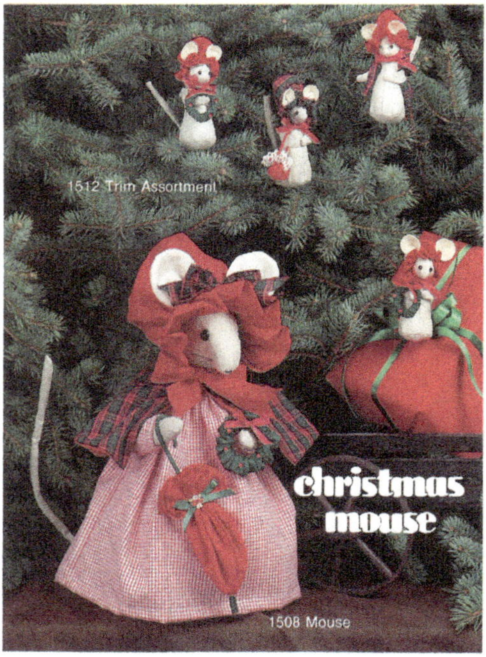
1512 Trim Assortment
christmas mouse
1508 Mouse

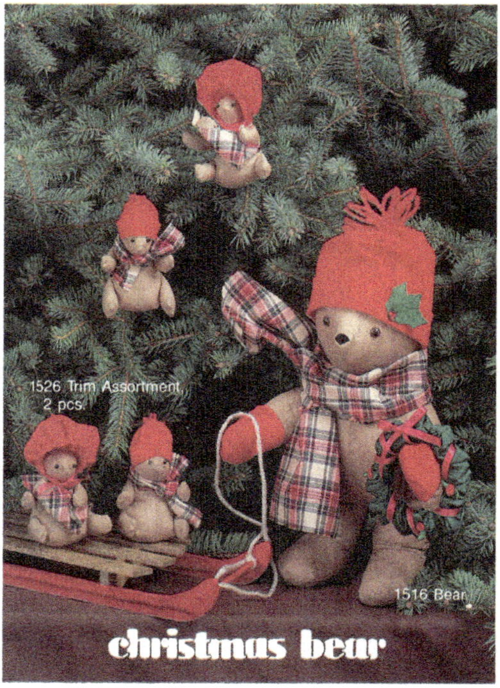
1526 Trim Assortment, 2 pcs.
1516 Bear
christmas bear

Overly-Raker, Inc.

Christmas, 1991

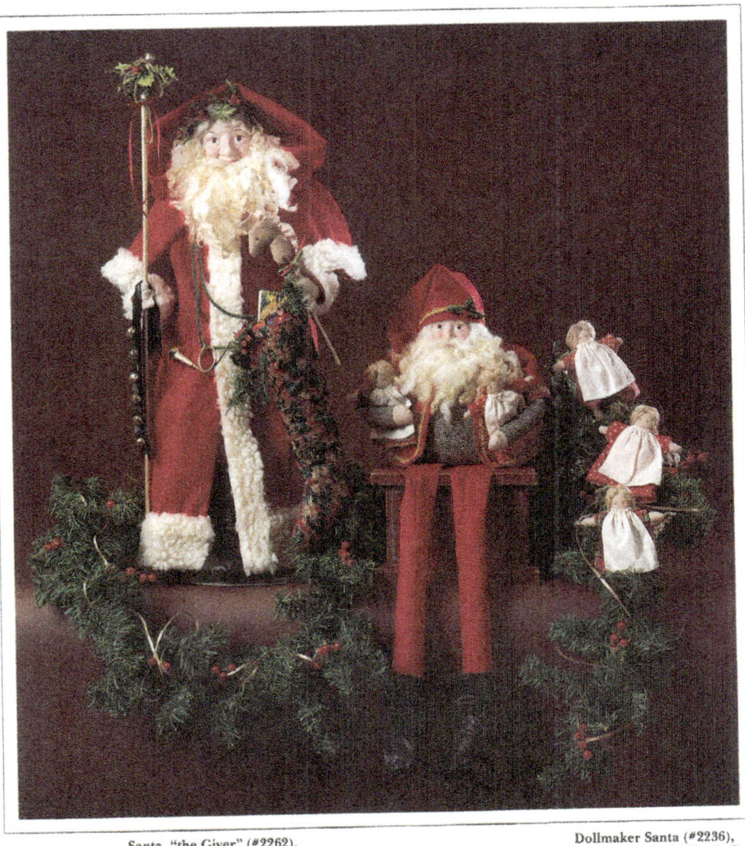

Santa, "the Giver" (#2262),
an original sculpture by Freda Raker.

Santa, "the Giver" has a handsome porcelain face and head, is 25″ tall and is bearded in beautiful natural uncarded Pennsylvania wool. He is dressed in a lined, shearling-trimmed red wool coat with a shoulder cape. Under his coat he wears red flannel underwear and boots. The Santa is a real doll with jointed fabric body so he will sit in a sleigh or chair. Along with his trimmed staff and bells he carries a Christmas stocking brimming with gifts.

Santa, "the Giver" is produced in a Limited Edition of only 150 and is hand signed by the artist. *FredaRaker*

Dollmaker Santa (#2236),
an original sculpture by Freda Raker.

This doll has a wonderful smiling face and head of porcelain. Our **Dollmaker Santa** carries two dolls and will sit on a mantel or shelf. He is bearded in beautiful, natural uncarded wool from Pennsylvania and is approximately 24″ sitting.

The doll trims (#1705) are available separately.

CHAPTER 19

Over the Next Few Years

The Irene Mae Company: Keep Focused on the Core Business

As if we did not have enough going on with running a successful wholesale and retail business, we decided we should expand into another business. The Home Party Plan was especially interesting to Freda. So with her urging, we decided to embark on a new small company called the Irene Mae Company. The name? Easy. We would just use our middle names for this new venture. My middle name, Irene, and Freda's, Mae. Thus, the new company was born in August 1983. Where to start? We had a very creative and energetic young man working for us at that time, Ray Davis, whom we put in charge to develop this project.

Let me back up just a minute. This home-party-plan company sprang from the fact that Freda and I had spoken at a couple of church functions and took samples of our products. Before we left that evening from speaking, all the ladies wanted to buy our samples. It was interesting. There was great enthusiasm with these ladies.

So now why not do a spinoff from Overly-Raker to the Irene Mae Company? Easier to say than do. There needed to be catalogs printed (two for demonstrators and smaller ones for prospective customers to take home), order blanks printed, pricing to be formulated, prizes to be given away, commissions, schedules to be made, but most importantly, women who wanted to be demonstrators and run their own little business to be contacted. A bigger project than we had anticipated. However, with Ray's leadership and endless hours, Irene Mae was launched.

It was fun and exciting and what I call moderately successful. But you can't serve two masters. The truth is, my enthusiasm faded since it was taking more of my time than I thought it was worth. We ran that little company for two and half years and then decided to close it. Some of our demonstrators were sorry to see it go since they were doing well. The biggest deciding factor to close was that Ray was leaving us and moving to another business. So ends the chapter of Irene Mae.

Moving On... and Accolades Follow 1984 State Employer of the Year Award

Overly-Raker was honored as the State Employer of the Year at the State Business and Professional Women's Convention. The nomination was submitted without our knowledge by the Lower Huntingdon BPW. A local newspaper article quoted an interview:

> We at *The Valley Log* are impressed by the unaffected nature of Freda Raker and Helen Overly. Freda gave the best answer as to why they were successful.
>
> "The Lord has done it through us, we haven't. The people who work for us are responsible in big measure for the success part. They are just great. The community and our employees have been very supportive of us."

We took seventeen of our employees with us to the State Convention at the Philadelphia Marriott to accept the award. It was a formal affair, and we all got dressed up for the occasion and had a terrific time. We were told, most often, only one or two employees accompanied the recipient. We were very proud to have several of our folks there.

This is a news release issued May 21, 1986, by Saint Francis College:

Overly-Raker Wins Small Business Award!

Helen Overly and Freda Raker of Overly-Raker Incorporated, were honored with the "Small Businesspersons of the Year" award at the Seventh Annual Small Business Development Center Symposium held at Saint Francis College on Wednesday, May 21.

This prestigious award was presented at a luncheon by Susan Garber, State Director of the Pennsylvania Small Business Development Centers. May 19–24 has been declared "Small Business Week" by President Ronald Reagan.

By 1983, Overly-Raker firm has become a nationwide $1,000,000 plus wholesale business. Their client list includes Carolina Soap and Candle, Procter & Gamble, First National Bank of Chicago, Girl Scouts of America, Freline Corporation, Hedstrom Corporation and Fabergé. Their products are currently available through Country Living, Country Notebook, J.C. Penney's, gift trade shows, permanent sales rooms and sales representatives.

The firm has also manufactured a limited edition Elvis Presley Doll, a Clark Gable doll, Christmas stockings for dogs, and have completed items for Penney's Christmas Catalog.

Overly-Raker currently manufacturers over 700 different soft-sculpture items and employs 35 full-time and over 200 part-time women who sew in their homes.

CHAPTER 20

Penn State and Production Ideas

Our business had grown steadily until 1985, when we had our first year of declining sales. I remember we told our employees that we probably were not going to be able to give them a raise and we would understand if they needed to go elsewhere to work, but not one of them left us.

In early 1986, I replied to a mailing by John Davis, who then worked with Pennsylvania small businesses for the Penn State University's Industrial Research office. The mailing suggested ways to help small businesses. Because of my reply to the mailing, John, in turn, talked to Dr. Kenneth Knott of the Department of Industrial and Management Systems Engineering. Knott saw the Overly-Raker situation as a study opportunity for a class taking his 1986 fall semester course.

Before we knew it, we had three student teams visiting the Overly-Raker production plant in McConnellsburg. Mr. Knott was correct; it was a great opportunity for the students and certainly a benefit to Overly-Raker.

When the first group of students came, I gave them a tour, showing them the departments: data processing, product development, design, cutting, sewing, silk-screening, stuffing, closing, kit making, training, quality control, and shipping.

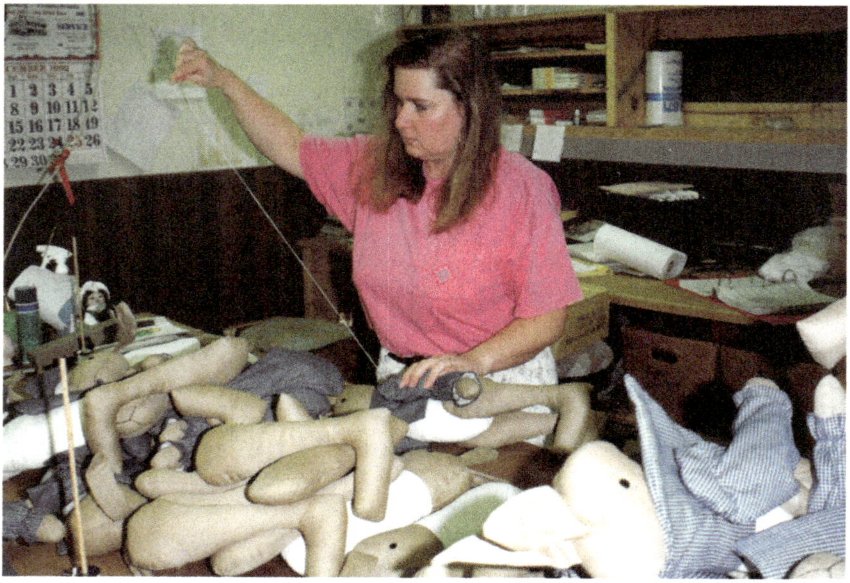

Pam Hollenshead making bunnies

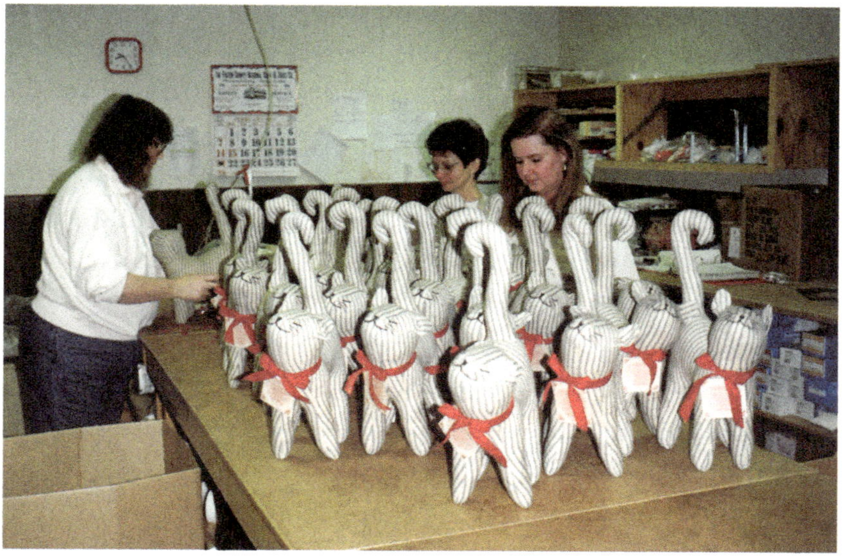

Cats, cats, and more cats

By December 1986, the students presented us with a five-year facilities plan, a productivity-improvement project, and a production control system that included an evaluation of commonly available control software for personal computers.

We had always taken pride in a very organized production line, but fresh eyes looking at the whole situation and a professor, Mr. Knott, who had years of experience in production, were just what we needed.

Freda and I were delighted with all three reports. The production control system that we call CJO (continuous job order) helped us the most. Overly-Raker was working so much smarter. The workers saw it and loved it.

I referred to all this to say we were blessed to have the opportunity for improvement in production. In 1986, Overly-Raker sales rose from $400,000, nearly 40 percent, to $1.4 million. In 1987, the sales topped at $1.7 million, and further expansion was imminent. Remember 1985, when we couldn't give our employees a raise? Fast-forward to 1987, when we paid our employees two bonuses plus an annual increase. That was the first time Overly-Raker would ever have two bonuses in one year, and that made Freda and me really happy. We often said we "became successful" and "we would rather be successful than rich." We know the difference.

In March of 1988, Penn State's Harlan Berger wrote a report for Overly-Raker, summarizing the strides to increase productivity:

> Three 5-student teams visited Overly-Raker's plant north of McConnellsburg on Route 522. The Fulton County accent hints of the Southern mountains. A converted two-story milk-processing building houses O-R's executive offices, production departments, and an outlet store that visitors find irresistible.

In December, 1986, Knott's students presented a five year facilities plan, a productivity improvement project, and a production control system that included an evaluation of commonly available control software for personal computers.

Overly was delighted with all three reports. "The production control system that we call the CJO—continuous job order—helped us the most; its impact has been unbelievable. It's a computer program that tracks each order and each product and each part of that product through the shop. Each morning we get a new 30-day printout. Every afternoon at 2:00 all department heads send their production figures to data processing. We know where everything is. The CJO is inventory control production control, and sales projection rolled into one. We now complete each order in about four weeks."

Overly points to a printout the thickness of the Wall Street Journal. On 10/06/1987, 96 of the pilgrim woman, home assembly, were at the home sewers and 24 in stuffing. Job order number and date was 09/18/1987; ordered were 144. Ninety-six of 144 shawls for the pilgrim woman were with part-timers. Of another 155 pilgrim women, 112 were in the kit room to be packaged for home sewers, 48 with the home sewers, and 28 in stuffing.

"We made some improvements of our own, but none was as important as the CJO," says Overly. "It has meant a 22 percent increase in productivity and a 36 percent increase in sales with the same number of workers. Since we didn't use the CJO until January—our year runs from May 1 to April

30—that improvement came about in little more than six months.

"Our accountants couldn't believe their figures. They grumbled that there must be some mistake. But there wasn't. Overtime in the stuffing room dropped dramatically, and cutting also pared overtime especially during the busiest months of August, September, October, and November, when we often have three UPS trucks in to load each day. The dinosaur order? We completed that $21,000 job in six weeks on top of regular business. Couldn't have done it before the CJO, absolutely not."

The CJO's impact was even more startling because the company spent virtually no extra money to implement it. Overly-Raker's data processing people wrote the CJO software for computers they already had. "I spent about $2000 to cover the students' travel and report costs," explains Overly, "and I made that up in a month or two. We're working so much smarter now. The workers see it and love it. I've told other local business people that they ought to ask for a team from Penn State. Everyone was professional; we were all delighted with your young people."

In 1985, O-R had grown to the point that the workers could barely cope. Helen Overly believes that the scary drop in sales was the best thing that happened to them. "This is not the usual business. We sell about 6500 accounts, most of them small. They range from $300 to $500. So we often didn't know where things were, and we spent too much time looking. We might have everything for the soft bear except the little hat, so the bear waited and might be forgotten. Everything depended on cutting; cutters would cut lots of one piece, then move on to another. Cutting was efficient that way but nothing else was. The continuous job order breaks that dependency on cutting and what we lose in cutting efficiency we gain a hundredfold throughout the plant. Cutting now cuts only enough for one day or what we can put through the plant in three days at the most."

The CJO also helps alleviate the frustrations of trying to integrate part-time production within plant operations. Every department head can see where orders are and how each is split between plant and home workers. In the kit room where components are compiled for home sewers, a digital scale blinks red: 0430. Exactly 48 beady eyes in the soda-bottle capful atop the scale. Precise and much quicker than counting eyes for the bears kits.

In stuffing, twin machines tumble white polyester fiber past windows reminiscent of laundromat machines. "Skins" sewn at home or by the three plant sewers come here. Air hisses as women hold the fabric skins over nozzles. Geese, bears, and draft dodgers (short-bodied critters whose long legs are stuffed under doors to stop cold air) swell. Each week about 3,000 pounds of polyester inflate O-R sit arounds.

Outside the stuffing room, a closing worker sews shut the nozzle holes, and the properly rounded creatures go to quality control. Those required to sit upright receive a dose of coarse sand from a red funnel one might use to change oil.

Quality control and packing take them next and from there they glide down a chute to warehousing.

Paul Orr, now a quality assurance engineer with Keystone Carbon was on the team responsible for plant layout. He enjoyed the experience for its blend of theory and practicality and says that Knott's class was the most useful of his Penn State courses. Orr's team focused on improving materials flow and recommended steps that would reduce travel distances of the three main product groups by 37 percent and increase warehouse storage 30 to 40 percent. A new drying system for silk screening would expand those capabilities by 533 percent. The Plant Layout Alternative report written by Orr, Sandy Super, Doug Francis, Tracy Elliot, and Craig Egli won a 1st Place Regional Award plus a 2nd place National Prize from the Institute of Industrial Engineers. It contains dozens of flow process charts, plant layout schemes, and cost estimates for various options.

Knott isn't surprised that Overly-Raker was happy with the results. His focus is on communication, both verbally and in writing or drawings. The consequences of miscommunication by an engineer are much more immediate and drastic. Knott's been doing these student-business projects for the past ten years and estimates that the 200 projects have saved each client $5,000 to $10,000.

CHAPTER 21

The *Law* That Changed the Business

Business was good, everyone was happy, both customers and employees, but suddenly we hit not just a bump in the road, but we ran right up against a mountain. On a perfectly lovely day in May 1989, a young man went into our office, asked for me, and proceeded to tell me that we were in violation of a 1937 state law. He first said, "I understand you make dolls," and I replied, "Not really." We made all kinds of soft sculpture, but not dolls, specifically. He then said, "I understand you have people who work in their homes." "Yes, we certainly do" was my reply. He informed me that we would have to cease and desist *today*. Wow, what a shock. "Cease and desist today." That would put a huge wrinkle in our production and maybe even put us out of business.

Let me explain what was done in the homes in our community. We did all the cutting of materials in the plant. The items (cut pieces) were counted, usually in packets of forty-eight, and a kit was made up with thread, cut pieces, and if necessary, components to be attached to the item. Women, and sometimes men, would come in, pick up one or two kits, whatever they wanted to do, take them home, sew, bring them back sewn into what we called skins. From there, the skins would go into our stuffing area, where we had automatic stuffing machines with one or two women stuffing, with high-quality polyester. From there, the item went into another department, where it had to be closed. That singular opening left open in the skin in order to be stuffed naturally had to be closed. Follow the item now to the finishing department, where it might have to have ribbons put on or any kind of attachment, like pretty little baskets, bells, hats, anything that might enhance the item dictated from the design department. We had five to eight women (depending on the season) working in the finishing area and checking quality control.

Back to the law. The 1937 union law prohibited the use of homeworkers in an effort back then to eradicate exploitation of the workers and to discourage the use of child labor.

Who knew that there was an old Pennsylvania state law that said you may not work for any one person in the home unless you're handicapped? In other words, a woman who worked with us in the home could work for us plus work for someone else, and everything would be fine, but she could not work exclusively for us in the home *unless she were handicapped.*

There were times we had over one hundred people working in the home. Who knew about this law? I will tell you. How did it come about that they found us?

I was asked, and I did speak about home-based businesses in seminars for Penn State University and University of Maryland. We started our business in our basement and grew a successful business; thus, we were a good example. We were happy to tell our success story and did not just tell them a story, but told everyone exactly what we did, how we timed the pieces, how each person was paid per piece, and explained it in great detail. We thought it was wonderful and were glad to share. That didn't turn out so well for us. I spoke in Philadelphia for Penn State for the subject Sewing for Success and, as mentioned, gave them in great detail how we ran our business. It seems there was a lady there who had checked with the Department of Labor and Industry to check the laws on starting a business. When my lovely seminar was over, she went to the Department of Labor and Industry and said, "I would like to be able to do what Overly-Raker does." Question, who is Overly-Raker? That began an investigation of us, the people who worked with us, and a long ordeal that nearly put us out of business.

Bear in mind that Freda and I were aware of the federal homeworker's law, which said we could not make gloves or belts and a few other items. We were in complete compliance with that; we just never even thought about a state law.

When this young gentleman came to my office with the shocking news, I said, "Surely we can have some phaseout time, give us thirty days to see what we can do." He was a nice guy, and if you have to have bad news, he was the one to give it to you. He suggested I call Helen Friedman (never will forget her name), who was the person in charge of the Department of Labor and Industry in Harrisburg. He sat in my office while I called her. I explained our plight, that we really needed some of this production, and asked if we could we have a thirty-day phaseout. Her answer was "If I were you, I would go out and get machines, bring them in now, and have the ladies come in to your place of work." Sure sounded simple enough to her. Answer remained: cease and desist that day. Now what she didn't know was we didn't have room in our building for more industrial machines, and those who were working at home were either retired and didn't want a full-time job, didn't want to work outside the home, or had children at home and wanted to work at a time convenient to them.

All this happened shortly after noon on that fateful day. What should we do next? I called the senior management team together and told them what happened, and they, like us, said, "It can't be. This is ridiculous." Why did we all think that? I decided that we should get all the employees together and tell them the dilemma, or big problem. We took everybody to our lunchroom and had a powwow. I explained that we didn't know what was going to happen, and if we had to shut down for a time to regroup and they needed to get another job, we would certainly understand. We were floundering in unknown waters.

Yes, without saying, everyone was in total shock at this situation we were faced with.

We had orders to ship but needed more production to fill orders in-house. What to do? We scrambled, did the best we could, but finally had to close the production area for nearly six weeks. During that time, we had to change things. Find space for new sewing machines and more employees. We took out a wall, found some used sewing machines, had the area rewired for three-phase electric power, and did all kinds of rehabbing for the new production lines.

While doing all this, we let it be known in our gift-industry publications what happened and wanted customers to know why we were not able to fill orders. Through one of those magazines, a young man that we had known in the industry called us and said he had a sewing factory in China and he would be glad to help us if he could.

Oh no, we were so proud of making everything in south-central Pennsylvania that going offshore was not in our thinking. However, we did have orders we needed to fill, so after talking with him, we cut the fabrics in our plant like we normally did; packaged them up (as we would to send out to homeworkers); air-freighted them to China, where they sewed the skins; then air-freighted them back to us, where we stuffed them, closed them, put on the adornments, and then shipped them to our customers. The sewing was great, but we lost money because air-freighting anything at that time was very expensive. The only good thing was we were able to fill most of the orders we had committed to.

Back in the office, it was a sad state for us and our employees. Interesting, through it all, we made the *New York Times*, the *Philadelphia Inquirer*, and were even contacted by *60 Minutes* to come on the program. Although the law was obsolete, as I was told many times, "The law is still the law." We received flowers and cards and calls, all of sympathy. We even had two calls to donate money to fight the law. One was anonymous, and we found later that that company was doing the same kind of home work as we did, thus wanted the law changed. We had a group of lawyers who would take the case at no cost. Freda and I traveled to NYC to meet them, but after thinking it over and praying about it, we decided to not go that route. Our decision was made based on all the time we would have to spend working on litigation and not getting any production done to run the business. We needed all our energy and creativity spent figuring out how to keep Overly-Raker a viable business.

In the meantime, overhead costs kept coming, senior management folks were working, the office had to remain open, and little or no product was going out the door.

You understand that no product being shipped means no money coming in. That's the kind of stuff that will bring you to and keep you on your knees. Despite it all, we *knew* God was still in control and somehow he would see us through these dark days. That is what faith is; it makes us certain of the things we do not see!

Did we stop altogether trying to "right a wrong"? No.

Through our state senator and representative, we were given a hearing at the state's Department of Labor and Industry. We took four of the folks who had worked in the homes with us. They did a fantastic job at testifying. At the end of the hearing, one member of the hearing committee said, "We sure got our clock cleaned today," meaning they could not find anything wrong. Every idea suggested we could do to solve the problems was struck down by those ladies testifying. For example, it was suggested we have our own day care for moms who had small children and that would allow them to go to the plant and work. One of the workers there testifying quickly answered that idea, saying that her child was in the first grade and she wanted to be home to get her on the bus and be there when she got home. It was not a matter of child care for her. Nor was it a matter for those retired women who wanted to work at their own time discretion or time frame. In the end, the head honcho said, "Overly-Raker is good *but the law is still the law.*"

We were never fined or hurt in any way for "breaking the law." There were apologies and a promise to help us. Since they had investigated us in the community and looked at all our books, it was obvious we were law-abiding citizens. Ignorant of the old, obsolete law.

I interject here that two senators took on the case to change the law. They worked on a bill that never reached the Senate. They sent me the bill with changes to ask my opinion. They were getting close to something that would work but as mentioned it never got out of the committee, was never voted on. Remember, this is an old union law, and it was hard to get action on it. No action was taken.

The Help We Received!

They allowed us to have some of the people who worked for us in the home go to a doctor and get a certificate saying they were handicapped. Handicapped? How so?

Some of the older women, who loved sewing and going to the plant (it was a social thing for them), went to the doctor. A couple had a bad back, a couple had high blood pressure, etc. These people were given certificates to continue to work for us. They were not charged for the certificates, nor were we. As always, there is a fee for documentation and lots of red tape, but those were all waived for us. We appreciated it because, at that time, any help was wonderful.

As mentioned earlier, we did rehab part of the space in the building and brought in sewing machines. Unfortunately, that was not a very good solution. Why? We had former factory workers apply and hired. Here was the problem. They were used to sewing large shirtsleeves or dress sleeves, and now we were asking them to sew a sleeve maybe an inch or two in size. We found not everyone can sew those intricate little items. So what happened? We would have a person work maybe a week or two and, in frustration, give up and quit. Others stayed but were dreadfully slow, so while the payroll was going up, the production was not even close.

Freda and I were offered all kinds of help from other manufactures, especially those who developed products outside the United States.

Two, in particular, contacted us about manufacturing in Mexico. Sounded good, so off we went to Mexico to search out other possibilities. The first company was fairly good at sewing, but we had to send all the fabrics, stuffing, shipping cartons, etc., to them. That worked for about two orders, and then we found they were running out of materials, especially stuffing. Come to find out they were using our stuffing for another company. Again, not a viable solution! The second company we visited was not able to do what we required.

I guess the best we got out of that rabbit trail was a visit to two different areas of Mexico.

Meantime, back at the ranch (McConnellsburg), we were limping along. *Limping* the key word here.

All the while, offers were coming in from different companies in China. Amazing, once the word got out that we had used one factory for some sewing, we had calls and faxes from others, some of these folks we knew from being in the gift industry.

Bet you are wondering—did we go to China? We sure did. We had heard of horror stories of working conditions in China, so we wanted to see firsthand, if we decided to give any one of these folks an order, what the working conditions were. Actually, we were pleasantly surprised at the factories we visited. The factory was well lit, painted white, concrete floor. Everyone seemed pleasant and happy. I was surprised at most all the workers were in Western clothing. Many of the men in white shirts. I wondered how they kept them so clean, especially since, on our way to one factory, we passed a countryside where there was a stream and the folks were washing clothes in the stream. The whole thing was an eye-opening experience but not a bad one.

Finally, we decided to try manufacturing offshore. We were selective and only did the simpler designs. How did it work out? Nothing is easy, and there were problems with fabrics and quality control, but we finally did get production acceptable to us. We were still making our upscale items here. There seemed to be some light at the end of the tunnel, but it was not without huge problems, including financial problems.

What to do? Among the other "help" that the state gave us were two very nice accountants assigned to us. They spent several days looking at our financials, our programs, and anything that would give them a picture of our financial situation. Interesting, they were surprised to find, in their investigation, we had paid a quarter million dollars to the homeworkers in our area in one year. All legal, all were given 1099 tax forms. Are you remembering, instead of sending the work to the homes here, we were forced to send to the same work to China to have it sewn? If that makes sense to you, good, but it sure didn't make sense to us. Our government at work because of an antiquated union law, even a new law could not get to committee to be voted on. "The law is the law." That forever rings in my ears, whether the law makes sense or not.

It was finally determined by the accountants that we would not be able to keep in business unless we had an investor or sold stock in the company.

But hold on, we were not done yet. We were blessed to be in a small rural community that still had two community banks. Overly-Raker had been customers of both banks. They had seen this little fledging company grow into a success. Both banks knew us, knew of our dilemma with the law, etc., and both were sympathetic to our situation. Ultimately, both loaned us the money to keep us afloat week after week until we could roll out more product and bring in more revenue. When I say we barely squeaked by, that is an understatement, but we did.

Back to the accountants who said it couldn't be done. They were watching us weekly. While they were rooting for us, they were sure, in the "the real world" it could not be done. They didn't know the God who opened doors for us, touched the bankers' minds for wisdom to loan us money (even we thought maybe too much sometimes), a workforce that could not be beaten, and faith to believe all things are possible for us who believe. To be sure, it was a miracle. "The law may still be the law," but fortunately, we have a God who is bigger than an antiquated law.

The remark of one of the accountants later was "We knew you were never going to sell stock or allow an investor in." Do you think he observed two independent women who would not give up?

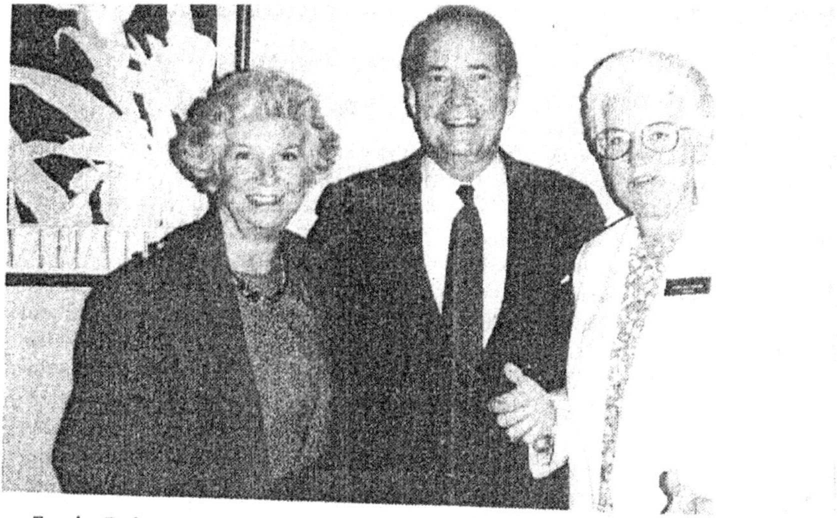

Freda Raker and Helen Overly, vice-president and president of Overly-Raker, Inc. of McConnellsburg pose with former Pennsylvania governor and U.S. Attorney General Richard Thornburgh during a September conference in Harrisburg. The 3rd Annual Pennsylvania Leadership Council conference featured the former Pennsylvania governor as well as former national "drug czar" William Bennett. The PA Leadership Council is a conservative grassroots movement designed to improve public policy in Pennsylvania. At last year's conference, Overly spoke in supoport of a Homeworker's Act which would ease restrictions on home workers in the job market. Thornburgh, a Republican, is running for a Pennsylvania Senate seat held by the late John Heinz, who was killed earlier this year in an airplane-helicopter accident. Thornburgh faces Sen. Harris Wofford in the election. Wofford is the former Pennsylvania Secretary of Labor & Industry appointed by Governor Robert P. Casey to fill the vacant seat until the election.

Printed with permission from Fulton County News

Harlen Berger wrote this reaction:

Overly-Raker, a small Pennsylvania business that was one of the largest producers of soft sculpture in the United States. At one time, 50 full time employees in the McConnellsburg plant and 150 part-timers working in their homes sewed and stuffed cloth skinned dinosaurs, geese, ducks, and sit-abouts, and decorations. Most of the sewing was done by home workers, a fact that brought home the companies Achilles heel. Fourteen months later in May 1989, the Pennsylvania Department of Labor and Industry nearly put Overly-Raker out of Business. The Department cited the industrial home-work law passed in 1937 that prohibits industry from contracting work to people at home, except to those who hold a physician certificate attesting to their handicap status. No grace period was allowed. In the next six weeks Overly-Raker lost 90 percent of its production and two-thirds of its work force. For two months, Overly-Raker turned heaven and earth, tearing out walls, running new 3-phase electrical lines and installing 30 sewing machines. Then the company discovered it couldn't find or keep help. Out of 58 people hired, 18 stayed. People who had made clothing, and there were a few in McConnellsburg, didn't want to sew the small intricate pieces of O-R products. Only 3 of the former home workers would come to the plant. Most had children and no transportation or simply wanted to work at home. In testimony given in Harrisburg, the women say that their paychecks were vital to family finances. Only 10 of the original home workers were certified as handicapped and continue to sew for Overly Raker.

By August, orders delivered had dropped by 20 percent, and the company had received its first shipment of 8,000 pieces sewn in China. Overly didn't want to send work overseas but saw no other way to fill her Christmas orders. She and Raker had considered and discarded many contingencies, such as moving to Maryland. But the overseas work didn't contribute much to profitability. By the end of 1989, the company's books showed a huge loss, much of it attributed to employee training.

McConnellsburg and surrounding Fulton County symbolize small town and rural Pennsylvania. Steady paychecks are few, so it is ludicrous to send any, let alone 100 products, to China.

Earl Baker, Senator from Chester County, has introduced a bill in the general assembly to appeal the 1937 Industrial Home Work law and to legalize non-hazardous home work. Robert Jubelirer of Blair County, has co-sponsored the bill. One hopes for bipartisanship on something so commonsensical. Since Overly-Rakers part-timers have given such eloquent testimony for their wishful work, it's evident that management and worker objectives mesh well in this case. And there must be similar cases out there; Overly-Raker has been operating with home workers for a dozen years without knowledge of the 1937 law.

Let's hope that the new legislation the worker's flexibility act passes soon.

Despite It All, There Were Still More Awards to Come...

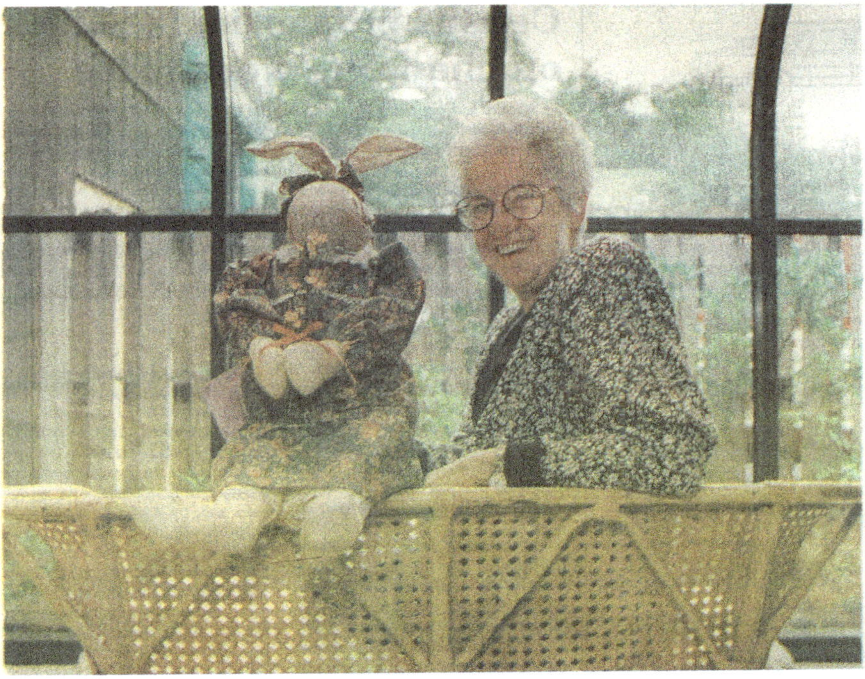

Business Leader of the Month

Employer of the Year was just one of the awards we received throughout the years. In October 1992, Overly-Raker was announced as the Business Leader of the Month in the *Herald-Mail.*

A pair of best friends and business partners are shaking up the gift industry with soft sculpture dolls that collectors are snuggling up to in a big way. Helen Overly, 60, the talker of the two, and

Freda Raker, 64, the creative inspiration behind the company, are celebrating 20 years as Overly-Raker Inc. From its humble beginnings in a basement workshop, the enterprise has grown to a 7,500 square foot manufacturing facility nestled at the top of Mercersburg Mountain. Overly-Raker creations are selling at a rate of $1.7 million a year and the delightful stuffed dolls are found in such mail order catalogs as JC Penney and Neiman Marcus. Upscale boutiques and gift shops also carry the specialty line. We were as green as grass when we started. Overly said of the partnership venture. The success of Overly-Raker is a story that goes beyond creativity and clever marketing. It's about fearlessness, drive and diversity. The company has survived a firestorm in the form of a Pennsylvania State Labor Law that nearly brought the business to its knees three years ago. Overly-Raker had depended on about 80 women sewing in their homes. But the state ordered a stop to that, citing a 1937 law forbidding work in the home, unless the workers are handicapped. With a backlog of orders, and seemingly no way to fill them, Overly said the company had to resort to having work done in China. "It was a nightmare, and I'm still not happy about it," she said. "I've always been opposed to offshore manufacturing." Overly has always been a big proponent of the buy American movement. "Unless we can use home stitchers, we must continue to import," she said. Overly said the home stitchers were women who welcomed the opportunity to earn money without leaving their homes. "Until this legislation is abolished, workers' flexibility will be limited," she said. Domestic sewing firms aren't interested in hiring themselves for small jobs, she said. Publicity surround the problem has gained Overly-Raker national recognition as the story gained local and national media attention, including a story in the New York Times. Today, 35 people work in the Overly-Raker factory, putting together the pieces that make the collectible Santas, nursery rhyme characters and other decorative soft sculpture dolls. In the early years, the company made "Realies," decorative collections of natural mushrooms and woodsy things that fit the environmental awareness mood of the 1970s. From there, the business moved to stuffed animals. Surprised and encouraged by the sales of their product, the two participated in the Chicago Gift Show and found yet more business. "The gift industry has been good to us." Overly said. "There are so many nice people." Overly now serves as the president of the Chicago Gift Show, one of the largest trade conventions in the country. The factory outlet store fronting the plant is a popular stopover for travelers looking for a bargain. While determination has kept Overly and Raker going all these years, the two also say that support from the community has helped them go the distance. Overly, a former junior high science teacher from New Jersey, and Raker, a former secretary for DuPont, have fun at what they're doing. They both say that imagination and humor will carry them into the future, and there's no telling what whimsy they'll introduce to the gift market next.

20th ANNIVERSARY

1973 - 1993

Overly-Raker, Inc.

".... still making friends."

A logo celebrating the milestone that others thought unattainable!

CHAPTER 22

Tent Sale Challenges and More Challenges!

Digging ourselves out of the hole from the Pennsylvania homeworkers law necessitated new ways for production.

So as you know, we had to bite the bullet and go to China to do some manufacturing. The challenge we faced was the volume we needed to order, sometimes container loads.

Here was the problem! If we were planning to bring out a new line of products when manufacturing in our plant here in McConnellsburg, we would make a limited number of pieces to bring to market. If the new items were a hit, great. We would immediately put them into production at our facility and build the inventory. If the new items were not great sellers, we stopped production. No problem.

However now we were having to order large quantities from China to have inventory *before* they had been tested in the market. That created a dilemma and, sometimes, fairly large mistakes by ordering more than what we needed. So here we were with a perfectly good product that sold less than we had projected. What to do with all the excess inventory filling our warehouse?

Not only did we sometimes overorder, leaving us with too much inventory, but oftentimes, the quality of the items that came to us was not up to our standard. So here was the challenge, what to do with overstock or less than perfect product.

We had friends visiting from Delaware, touring our overstocked warehouse. In discussing problem 1, as I remember, Cindy Brink, suggested a warehouse sale.

That clicked with me, but the logistics of having people in our warehouse to buy the product was impossible.

But enter a different idea: a tent sale! Oh, what an idea that turned out to be!

Since we had the big Fulton Fall Folk Festival event soon, bringing in hundreds of people into the county, why not have a tent sale then? Genius!

The sale was to be Friday and Saturday, nine to four, and Sunday, one to four.

Sure enough, we set about bringing the sale to fruition! Leon Hurst, who was the man in charge, loved the idea too. He went about renting a tent. Freda and I, along with Leon, looked at the inventory ledgers. Decisions, what to sell and at what price. The price was important because we needed to move the stuff. Realistically, we most often sold large volumes below our cost.

The tent was erected in our parking lot. Many of the employees became involved. Warehouse people had to move the product out to the tent in large cartons in a layout that allowed people to move around and shop. Office personnel made price lists and signs for each carton. Production people left their regular duties to help with the checkout line with customers. At the first sale, we had only one cash register. That turned out to be a mistake. Long lines grew. As the lines backed up, we had an additional person with just a calculator adding up the sales and checking people out. At each checkout, we had a bagger helping to move the checkout more quickly.

Oh yes, and about the bags. One of us, who knows who, had the foresight to provide bags for the shoppers. Leon, the purchasing agent, ordered clear large plastic bags for the shopper. Treva Starr, one of our top sewers, took charge of welcoming shoppers at the entrance of the tent and offered each person a bag. Often, people would say "No, thank you," only to come back after they saw the bargains and ask for a bag.

Brenda Taylor, supervisor of the cutting department, now headed up the cash registers and checkout lines.

Was that tent sale idea a success? What I have just written about was the first sale. That was only a beginning. Each year, the sale got bigger with many more customers. The fifth and last year, we had five cash registers and a separate tent only for checkout, with nearly all our personnel working in or about the tent.

The Overly-Raker Tent Sale became one of the highlights of the Fulton Fall Folk Festival. It was a major player in the festival events. People would line up early in the morning to be first in the tent for bargains. Freda and I went an hour early and could not even get in to park. People were lined all across the parking lot.

It became a mark of stamina just to survive the tent sale. We had stickers made up, saying, "I survived the Overly-Raker Tent Sale," and would place one on the customers as they checked out. We had four thousand stickers made up, and they were all gone by Sunday morning.

Fortunately, we had great success; emptied out excess inventory, making room for new, good, saleable product; and freed up money to move forward.

Never give up! As my nephew, Ron Menhorn, used to say, "Never a problem, only an opportunity." That was always our attitude. Armed with faith, trusting that somehow God would give us guidance and an opportunity to show him strong on our behalf. He never failed!

CHAPTER 23

How Do You Know When to Let Go?

Rebuilding the business after the "law" problem was challenging, hard work, an uphill climb, but fun! Success, no matter how small, is always exciting. Digging out of a hole and seeing some light creates enthusiasm to climb on. Climb on we did, as always, with help from loyal employees, good sales reps from Shannon Marketing, and of course, Overly-Raker customers.

Freda and I talked about how blessed we were and continually thanked the Lord for this. But did you ever notice, as we walk by faith, God seems to put yet another faith test in our path? Uh-oh, what now?

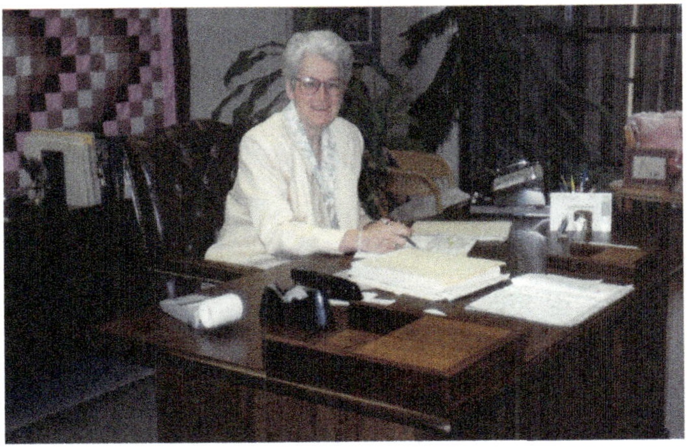

The chief

Because we had to do some manufacturing offshore (competition mandated), we were introduced to several Chinese manufactures. Freda and I became friends with a young man who lived in Wisconsin but owned sewing facilities in China. He had done selected work for us at one of his factories. He had watched our business grow.

He contacted us and asked to meet with us. The reason? Unbelievable. He wanted to buy our company. Wow! The company was not for sale. As months went by, we had lots of discussions regarding this idea of selling the business. If you are reading this and have started and grown a business, it is quite like raising a child. How do you give it up?

More months of talk between us and the other administrative staff and department heads of Overly-Raker. We labored over the pros and cons. We had lots of discussions. We took into account our ages and the uphill climb necessary for us, considering the debt we had incurred when we went through the "law" adventure.

What to do?

Jonathan, the persistent, unrelenting, determined buyer, did not give up easily and finally presented us with a buy/sell proposal. We, in turn, took the proposal to the lawyer and to an accountant, who had lots of experience with guiding folks through buying and selling businesses.

Now all this time, I admit I thought it was pretty neat, flattering too, that someone would want to purchase our business. I went through the motions, but in fact, deep down inside, I didn't want to sell.

The day of reckoning came. All the changes we made to the sales contract were accepted, no negotiation. But for me, "Wait, I want talk about it more." But my dear partner, Freda, said firmly, "I want to sell."

So there it was. Sell!

December 31, 1996, was our last day as full-time entrepreneurs. It was a wonderful twenty-three years. The gift industry was not only a good place for a business but also the best place to meet and make wonderful friends.

Our employees, the best! No finer, more loyal people ever existed. More than anything, our concern was that they would continue to have employment. We were assured all would be the same as far as employment was concerned.

Manufacturing would be the same, sales group the same, and location would remain in McConnellsburg. So there it was, the selling of our beloved business. Freda and I had a three-year employment contract to continue to work for the company and see it through a transition. As good as the prospects are, the promises made, the good intentions, I have learned that transferring a business from the original owners, who built the business, to a new entity just isn't the same. Rarely does it work out as expected. Overly-Raker was to be in the latter statistic.

The buyer's intentions were good. He had invested in several businesses but was not a hands-on owner. However, the person he hired to run the business in his absence had a different plan. The new owner operated larger businesses in the Midwest and visited Overly-Raker only once or twice a year. Unfortunately, all the good plans seemed to falter in many areas of the business. The person he left in charge had his own ideas for design etc. Sales were down because the designs no longer looked like Overly-Raker. True, our products had a distinctive look. Salespeople told us that customers did not like the look of the new designs. Therefore, they did not buy them. Actually, Freda and I had had gotten out of our contact since the person in charge didn't allow us to do much, and the situation became rather uncomfortable. Finally, after two years, it came to light that the new owner, Jonathan, had been feeding the company money to keep it running but it had finally come to an impasse. He said he would have to close the company because he could no longer keep it going. He came to us with that message and also asked us to let him out of the lease he had in our building.

Apparently, there had been a lot of misinformation given to him and to us in the beginning through his representative. Our biggest worry was our employees, who would now be out of work. However, in quick time they were all able to find other jobs. Thus, sadly, Overly-Raker was an end of an era.

Now you know the story of Overly-Raker. You must know now too that the company motto, "We make friends," surely does describe Helen Overly and Freda Raker.

Founders Step Down

Not retirement, just a change of pace for Helen Overly and Freda Raker founders of Overly-Raker. The partners will be leaving the Company on a full time basis at the end of the year, December 31, 1996. To quote Helen, it's been a wonderful 23 years. The gift industry is not only a good place for business but the best place to meet and make wonderful friends. If you know Overly-Raker you will know too, the motto of the company, WE MAKE FRIENDS. Helen and Freda have surely lived up to that motto, with friends all across the country. Ask Freda, will you miss the business? A resounding "yes and especially all the friends we have made over the years." What is ahead for the business partners? They may still be doing some of the shows in general as (how is this for a title) ambassadors-at-large for the Company. (*Fulton County News*, January 1997)

CHAPTER 24

Now for the Rest of the Story of Two "Brave Hearts"

Suddenly, here we are with lots of free time. What to do? A bit scary when we had been used to being very busy running a business with hardly enough hours in the day to get everything done.

For me, it was also time to resign from the Board of the New York International Gift Fair since I was no longer in business. As I spoke with Jeff Little, the show director for NYIGF and CEO of GLM Inc., he asked what I was going to be doing. As an aside, this GLM was the company that Mr. Bill Little introduced me to back when we began in the midseventies.

My reply was "I don't know, but you can be sure I will be doing something."

With that he suggested that I wait just a bit and perhaps I could work for them, part-time. Now that was exciting for me. It would keep me in the industry that I loved, and I would have a "job" to look forward to.

The job I finally began in the spring of 1997 with GLM was a buyer's service representative. What a great job. I visited gift shops, museums, and any place that sold gifts in Pennsylvania, Maryland, and DC. And even better, I attended all the major trade shows throughout the country that GLM owned then; that included gift, stationery, textile, aromatherapy, and gourmet and houseware shows. Who could ask for anything more?

GLM Appoints Buyer Services Representative

> George Little Management has appointed Helen Overly to the position of Buyer Services Representative. Overly will be responsible for further development of GLM's relationship with buyers in the gift industry with a focus on the Mid-Atlantic Region. Overly brings 20 years' experience to the gift industry to this position. Most recently she was the President and CEO of Overly-Raker Inc., a soft-sculpture company she co-founded 23 years ago. (Quote from a GLM press release, September 1997)

In the meantime, back at the ranch. Freda was already busy developing new techniques for sculpting with clay and creating new designs. She was able to travel with me to a few shows and actually worked with the company, Catherine Lilywhite, both designing and working at the booth, helping with sales.

But as always, when God closes a door, he opens another. In our case, it was the beginning of a whole new adventure.

CHAPTER 25

Why I Volunteer Support the Community That Supports You!

> These two women have been involved in community projects almost since they started in business.
>
> —Cheryl M. Keyser, *Public Opinion* newspaper

Involvement in the community has always been important to both Freda and me. It seems a good "payback" for support from the community.

On December 8, 1988, *Fulton County News* reported this:

> Helen Overly, president of Overly-Raker, Inc. has been elected president of the board of directors of Fulton County Medical Center, the first woman to be elected to the presidency of that board... Ms. Overly has served as a board member and secretary since 1978. She is active in numerous organizations, including the Fulton County Chamber of Commerce, the Association of Retarded Citizens of Fulton/Franklin Counties and the Fulton County Tourist Promotion Agency.
>
> Ms. Overly is vice president of the Chicago Gift Show, the largest gift show in the nation. She

> also serves on the board of directors of Mantec, York County, PA, an industrial resource center affiliated with the University of Pennsylvania that assists Pennsylvania businesses in manufacturing technology.

After we had sold our business and while I was working part-time for GLM, I was asked to volunteer as the chair of a fund-raising committee for a new hospital. There had been talk of building a new hospital for several years, but little action had been taken. A local businessman and his wife, Andy and Joyce Washabaugh, had donated twenty acres for this new project.

How did I get involved, and why would I ever think of volunteering?

Recently I was asked that question, "Why did you volunteer, or what made you volunteer for a fundraising job?" Interesting story. I'll start from the beginning!

I received a call from the CEO, Bob Murray (2002), of our local medical center, inviting me to go to his office. He would like to talk with me. He and the CFO, Jason Hawkins, met with me to ask if I would chair the fund-raising committee for a new hospital. There had been a lot of talk for a few years about a new hospital. Now, apparently, they were ready to go.

My very first thought was, number 1, I had no experience in fund-raising, nor did I want to find out about it. Number 2, I was way too busy with many other things on my plate to consider taking on this job.

As we talked, I asked, "How much do you have to raise?" $1.5 million. What I didn't know until after I finally volunteered was that the board had previously done a feasibility study and was told that we could raise $1 million, maybe 1.5 million. Interesting, that was the amount they said we had to raise.

I talked it over with Freda and family and good friends. All had the same conclusion. A resounding "No. You are way too busy to take on this task."

But I made the first mistake by telling the CEO I would think about it. That is the wrong thing to say. It leaves the door wide-open to being pushed through to a yes position.

I was leaving the next day for a trade show in Atlanta. I told him I would give him an answer when I got back.

I am a person of faith, and I prayed about it, asked for guidance and direction on what to do especially after such negative response from family.

Off I went to Atlanta for a week. I was busy there all week and, honestly, didn't think another thing about this. Actually, I completely forgot about it until I was on the plane coming home when it hit me. Oh no, I had promised an answer on a specific date, and I had not given it any thought.

Because I promised a decision, I called the CEO to explain that I had not really given this proper thought. I was leaving for Washington, DC, the next day to work at another trade show. I said I would return in three days and then, for sure, I would give him an answer. This decision plagued me. What to do? It was tough to say no to such an important project, but even if I said yes, could I do it?

The answer became very clear in the most miraculous way.

While I was in Washington, Will Little, the president of GLM, the company that I worked with, flew in for three hours to attend a board meeting. After the meeting, he came into the office where I happened to be. We chatted a minute or two. He causally asked what I was doing these days. "Are you still on the board of the hospital?" "No," I said, "you're way behind times, Will. I have not been on that board for some years, but funny that you should mention the hospital. We [notice I said *we*] are going to build a new hospital, and they have asked me to chair the fund-raising committee. But I don't think I can do it. I am way too busy and know nothing about fund-raising." We chatted a bit, then he asked, "How much do you have to raise?" I replied, "Oh, about a million and a half." With that, he pulled his business card out of his pocket and said, "If you will do it, I will give you 1 percent." Wow! I saw $15,000 flash in front of my eyes. I exclaimed, "Oh no, Will, now I have to do it." In the grand scheme of things, when building a hospital or anything, for that matter, $15,000 isn't much, but when you have nothing and you're offered $15,000, it's huge.

Suddenly I realized I had my answer. Unless God had written it on the wall, could the guidance I had prayed for been made more clear? Interesting to note, Will Little knew no one in Fulton County except Freda Raker and me. It really was a gift to us and to move me on to say yes.

Remember, Will Little had worked with me in Chicago, where I had a leadership position at the Chicago Gift Show. Thus, he believed (more confident than I was) I could do the job.

I came back to town and contacted Bob Murray with my answer! No more than when I said yes that the amount needed for the building project jumped to $3 million, and it didn't stop there; the target kept moving one more time to $6 million and finally landed at $7 million. That was until the Specialty Clinic was to be added and another million dollars was raised.

Hard to believe we could raise that amount of money from this small rural County.

I had a wonderful, hardworking little committee (team) that touched people with very big, giving hearts that made it possible to meet the goal and build a wonderful facility. Where to start?

I read everything I could about fund-raising, talked to anyone with even a small amount of experience, and set off to garner a committee. I decided we would need folks from every part of the county who knew the people and neighbors there whom they could contact. Not genius on my part, but it was so right! Then I was blessed to know a fund-raiser, Marge Taylor, who gave me a lot of information and, even better, introduced me to a retired professional fund-raiser, Paula Callery, who was so gracious to give of her time and talent, for free, to me.

I had some good information from the Internet, but she enhanced all the information I had gathered. I played with all kinds of numbers, considering our population count (fourteen thousand). How much would each one have to give to reach our goal? How many people could we find for large gifts. $50,000 and up? Who would they be? Yikes, what a job I had gotten into. I hate to ask for money in the first place, and now how would I be bold enough to ask for $50,000, $100,000, and more?

A couple of interesting stories.

We had just gotten started, had a big sign erected ("Future Site of Fulton County Medical Center") on the location of where the new facility would be built. That got attention that we were serious about building this hospital.

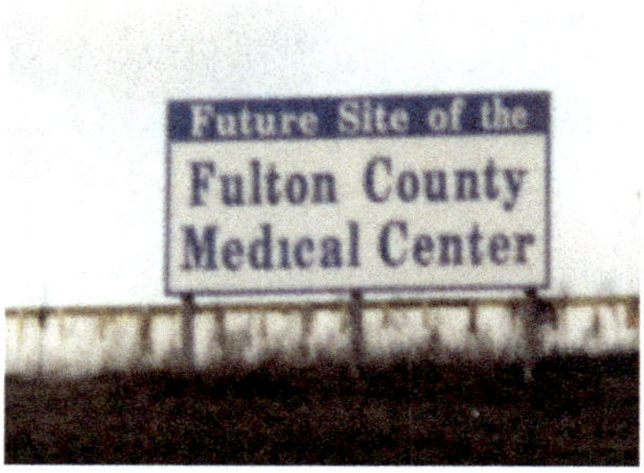

The vision

I received a call from a local banker. Could I go in and talk with him about someone who wanted to donate a sizable gift to the start of the building fund? Oh boy, could I go in? You bet, in fifteen minutes. My head was spinning. Wonder how much money he was talking about. Maybe $10,000, $25,000?

I went to the bank, and after some talking the banker, John Duffey told me the individual wanted to donate (hold your hats and pocketbooks) *one million* dollars! I thought we were nearly home free.

But wait a minute, not so fast. Turned out this gentleman began talking to his "buddies," who were extremely skeptical that we could raise enough money to build a new hospital. He was told by his buddies that he would be throwing good money after bad. So he decided he was not going to donate the million. Bad news. A huge disappointment. But not to be deterred. I decided it was time for the first sales job persuading the donor to come back on board. After the CEO and I made a couple of visits with the potential donor, he was persuaded that we actually could and would build the hospital. I give credit to his sister, Catherine "Tat" Shimer, for our success. She encouraged him to make that affirmative decision. Thank you, John Shimer.

The second story is my favorite. I talked with this gentleman about our need for his help. After spending time reiterating facts and figures, he agreed to give us $230,000. "Oh, but if you give us an additional $20,000, you can have a nice naming opportunity." Specifically, naming of the front lobby. He replied, "I don't care if my name is on the wall or not." I immediately retorted, "But your family would be proud." That didn't necessarily impress him, although he did not give me a definite no. He just smiled and left me hanging. As time went by, I visited him several times. With each visit, I brought up that larger figure (total $250,000). In my heart of hearts, I was sure he would untimely give that amount. So sure was I that this is what happened. We had a big kick-off event formally announcing our fund-raising capital campaign to the general public.

At that event, I had a young man, John Ott, pick up this gentleman and take him to the event. We had three donors who pledged $10,000, $20,000, and $25,000 to the campaign. Then I announced that the first big pledge of $250,000 came from our local philanthropist and businessman Ray Koontz. With that, amid all the cheers and clapping, he looked at the young man who had taken him, and said, "I never told her I would give her that." Aw, but be assured *he did.*

I know that was a very gutsy move on my part, but I also knew the heart of this man.

Now is fund-raising easy? An astounding *no*! However, if the project is very important, and a new hospital was, it is worth it all.

As time went by with our fund-raising, my committee and I were blessed to have a hardworking development expert hired by the medical center, Cheryl Brown, who brought with her a wealth of experience. She came to our aid with several new "tools" that helped us all, working together, get over the top!

If you are ever in the fund-raising business, it is not easy, has lots of hills and valleys, but depending on the project, it is very rewarding.

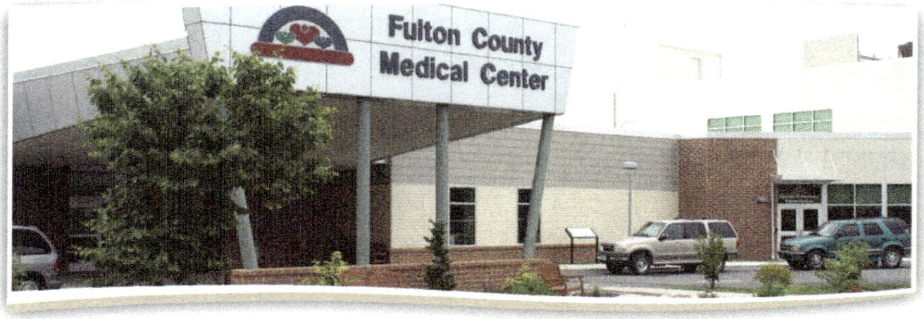

From vision to reality

CHAPTER 26

Memories of Freda

Freda, Freed, Aunt Freedie

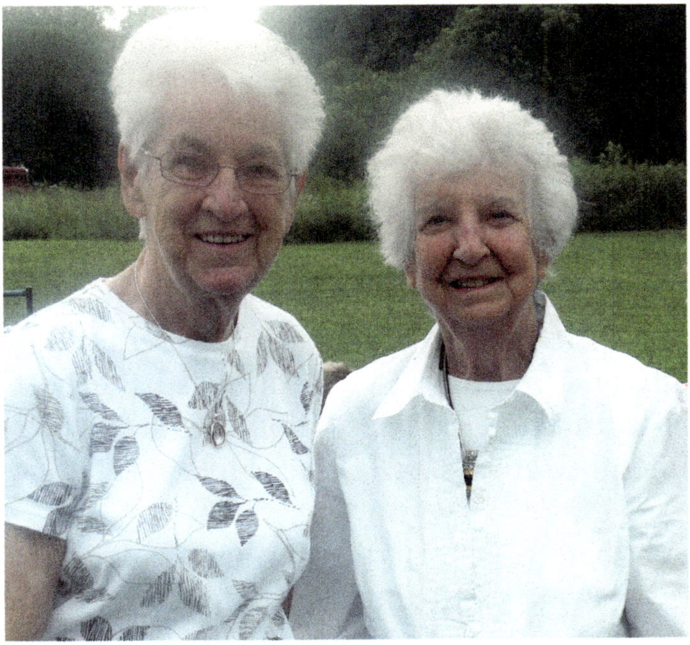

The partners

These are all names that bring special memories to this one person identified here in this story, Freda Mae Raker.

She was a classy lady in every sense of the word, loved and revered by friends and family alike.

While Freda had no children of her own, Aunt Freedie was a very special person to all her nieces and nephews, encompassing three generations.

Already you have gotten to know this creative, smart, extremely organized, talented, practical person that I very often referred to as the brains in this duo. She was able to look at a situation and make good decisions from an intelligent point of view, not an emotional one. While I have bragged about her qualities, she was not perfect. Like all of us, she had some quirks and idiosyncrasies we had to deal with. Stubborn would be one of those, but only after she had examined the situation from every angle. Her decision would be made, and then it was not negotiable.

A lovely personality, always gracious, ready to welcome all as friends. Because we both met and became friends with so many folks, it was just natural that we entertained a lot. There was always an open invitation at our house. Just as Freda was so creative artistically, so was she in the kitchen. She loved to try and experiment with all sorts of new recipes. Baking and desserts were her specialties, especially at Christmas. We always had the best-tasting and most unusual cookies, along with lovely dessert compliments to any dinner. (Since I like to eat, that worked for me.)

Freda had a special talent for seeing trends long before they came on the market. This was true in fashion, clothing, gift, or home design. This gift contributed greatly to the directions we took with our products.

She was the ideal business partner for me. No matter what I became involved with, in or outside the business, she was always in the background, with wonderful and logical ideas. In her own quiet way, she often pushed me to be even more involved than I may have been otherwise.

We had a great working partnership based on total mutual respect. Respect is the key word here. Her artistic instincts were, without question, exceptional. How easy it was for me to brag about her and easy to sell her designed products. I, on the other hand, had none of her talents but could use my own talents to promote, sell, and market the products. Totally different talent pulling in the same direction. We needed each other to complete the success story. Throughout all our years together, our business had its ups and downs; our lives were full of hard work, enriched by the fact that somehow we never lost our sense of humor and by our keen appreciation of each other's gifts.

To readers and to friends, we had a great, wonderful ride in business and with friends around the country. Indeed we did. Two county girls succeeded as entrepreneurs.

Our Lives Changed

However, in 2005, we were struck with a disease no one likes to face. Freda, whom, you will remember, I called the brains in this duo, began to have memory problems. She insisted, with her doctor, that she needed to seek more help. Upon an hour-long evaluation by a neurologist, she was diagnosed with "moderate benign memory loss." The good news was it was just "moderate" and she was able to function quite well with little or no help for a couple of years. But then the "moderate" became serious and went on to severe.

As time went by, the memory problems consistently got worse. If anyone knows anything about dementia/ Alzheimer's disease, unfortunately, for now, it is a losing battle. No cure yet.

Our dear Freda always had a pleasant personality. Therefore, as her condition deteriorated, she was easy to care for. We battled this dreaded disease together for seven years. In November 2012, we lost the battle.

What good came from this ordeal? Lots.

Out of Every Burden, There Is a Blessing

In Freda's memory, we started a support group for dementia/Alzheimer's caregivers at our local medical center. This has been so well received. Those who attend share their challenges and successes. What works for one case may not work for the other. We have found that each person has their own set of hurdles to get over. There is a lot of learning with becoming a person caring for someone with dementia.

There is no pill that can take away the problem or ease the pain for either the person with the disease or the person trying to take care of them.

What we have learned, collectively with the group, is we are not alone. Frustration is inevitable. Being overwhelmed at times is a natural thing. We sometimes feel a bit of guilt having unrealistic expectations, always wanting to do more. The list goes on and on, but together we share all the emotions that affect us. Bottom line, we have learned to live in the moment, to take care of ourselves and, by all means, keep a sense of humor.

We have learned also that we should not be trying to get our loved one to remember something. Sounds simple, but they are already suffering with trying to remember, and we just add to their frustration and stress when we ask them to *try* to remember.

I think back to the beginnings of this, saying to Freda, "Oh, surely you can remember that." In my mind, it was something very simple. It could be something common she had done repeatedly for years. To me, why could she not remember? It took a while to accept that her brain connectors were not connecting; therefore, what was simple a year ago was gone now.

Lest you think this caregiving is all hard and sad, let me assure you, once you accept the reality of the situation, you will have plenty of good times and lots of laughs.

Example at our house (this is one of her later stages), one evening after a bath and her teeth were brushed, Freda looked at me and smiled! Yikes, her teeth were all black, looked like she had no teeth.

"Freda, what did you do to your teeth?" Innocent as a very young child, she responded, "I didn't do anything."

For me, the scary thing was I didn't know what she had gotten into, maybe black markers or shoe polish or something that might be harmful to her. She was very surprised when I took her to the mirror. She immediately began to try to clean off whatever she had put on.

In the meantime, I ran upstairs to her bathroom and discovered the culprit: mascara. A tube with a brush. There you have it. Brushed her teeth with the little mascara brush.

Other brush stories. As time went by, I assisted her with brushing her teeth. I would put the toothpaste on the toothbrush, and if I was not watching her, closely, more than once, she brushed her hair with the first swipe.

Perhaps that seems sad to you, and it can be, but in the big picture, these are just funny little things that happened. It helped to see the bright side sometimes.

One of my favorites is the day I was down in the lower level, working at the computer.

Set the stage. It was Christmas, and we had three Christmas trees in the living room. Each tree was the tall pencil type about five to six feet tall!

I went up from the basement office and sat down in the living room. To my shock and dismay, I looked, and one of the trees was gone. It had been fully decorated with lights and all, and suddenly it was *gone*. Where and how? You guessed it—Freda had no idea.

Truth is she had unplugged the lights on the tree and carried it down to the basement and placed it back in a corner where I didn't see it at first look.

After some searching on my part, I found the tree and tried to get it back to the living room. Here is the best part. She got it down there and did not lose one single decoration. I, on the other hand, lost several on the way back up. She declared she had no part in the moving of the tree. She surely believed it to be so. Completely innocent!

The Support Group

Before I finish this chapter, I would like to mention again the support group we started. If anyone reading here and is dealing with this disease, find a *support group* in your area. It is so important finding others (caregivers) who can share ways to cope with and handle problems or successes when dealing with loved ones suffering with dementia/Alzheimer's.

What we do know from attending our support group is this. We as caregivers are not alone. We share lots of problems and sometimes have had similar things where we share a solution that worked for us and may help others.

An example: A huge problem for family members or caretakers is taking the car keys away from someone. Often, the person suffering will start out and forget where they are going or drive somewhere and not remember how to get back home. This is a very real problem.

In my case, Freda got into the driver's seat and said, "Now let's see, which is the gas pedal and which is the brake!" I really did not know she was that bad, but time to take away the keys. This was easier for me than it was for others. She didn't care to drive too much as I or someone was here to take her where she wanted to go.

I hear from other caretakers where there is a real battle over this. Some creative ways to solve the problems I have heard are disconnecting the battery, losing the keys, etc.

We hear many words of thanks and praise for this support group. Two staff people work with the group and plan speakers for each month. I rarely miss a monthly meeting and am there to help facilitate the meeting.

It has helped so many to cope with a difficult disease that produces very trying times in the daily lives of all.

As for me, and because I know Freda would want this, I am still very involved with the medical center that hosts the support group. Among other volunteer positions I carry out, I also serve on the board of Fulton County Medical Center Foundation.

EPILOGUE

Faith with Habakkuk

You have just been with me through a journey of the ups and downs of two unlikely entrepreneurs who quit successful jobs at ages forty-two and forty-seven to travel a faith route and, along the way, to be blessed with making friends in business across the country.

Faith has been the key through it all.

During the faith journey, our faith was made even more poignant as both Freda and I were taught a big lesson of patience and faith through the life of Habakkuk, a minor prophet in the Old Testament. Habakkuk talked with God regarding the terrible conditions of society (corruption, no justice, etc.) and was upset because God did not seem to answer. But God did answer.

God reminded Habakkuk that "the just (righteous) shall live by *faith*." Not by what we see or our circumstances at the moment but by trusting wholly in God. The dialog continued between the two until Habakkuk determined to quit talking and just sit and watch what God would do.

As time passed, Habakkuk began to enumerate all the great things God had done in the past. As he did this, his own faith began to build.

Just as in Habakkuk's experience, our faith became bolder though our business and life adventure. Faith, patience, and hope grew in great measure. We found God is never late, always on time; trust him. There is great joy in knowing God, when we move from doubt to faith and hope, going on beyond our daily experience to fully trusting God, no matter the circumstances.

The great final triumph came when the prophet, Habakkuk, began to praise God and (*my paraphrase*) said, no matter the circumstances or how bad things are, "yet I will rejoice in the Lord." That is real victory!

Even though (Bible reference, Habakkuk 3:17–18)

Though the fig tree does not bud and there are no grapes on the vines, though the olive crop fails and the fields produce no food, though there are no sheep in the pen and no cattle in the stalls, yet I will rejoice in the Lord, I will be joyful in God my Savior.

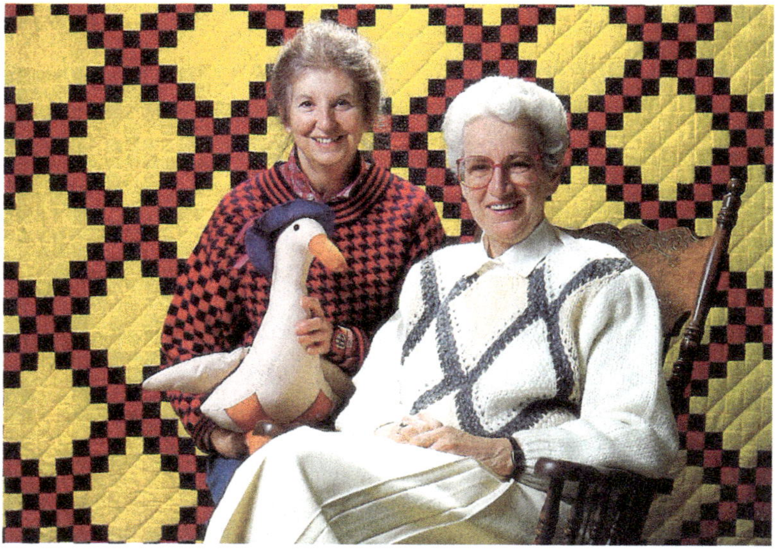

And rejoice we do!

CPSIA information can be obtained
at www.ICGtesting.com
Printed in the USA
BVOW11*1309071116
466373BV00004B/4/P

9 781635 244366